THE LANGUAGE GAME

THE LANGUAGE GAME

Inspiration and Insight for Interpreters

Ewandro Magalhaes

MAGELLANIC

Copyright © 2019 by Ewandro Magalhaes

All rights reserved. This book or any portion thereof shall not be reproduced or used in any manner whatsoever without the express written permission of the publisher except for the purpose of brief quotations in a book review.

The Language Game – Inspiration and Insight for Interpreters

ISBN 9781081899479

Proofreading by Samantha Vila

Published by Magellanic Press
New York, NY

info@magellanic.press
www.magellanic.press

To Mena, with all my love.

And when this sound occurred, the multitude came together, and were confused, because everyone heard them speak in his own language.

Acts 2:6

Disclaimer

This book is a compilation of articles written and published over the last twelve years. Some of them have been recycled from previous talks and chapters of a book released in Portuguese. I have revisited and blown new life into them, but nearly all articles here can be found online for free, though not in the same form.

Ewandro Magalhaes brings you into the booth and behind the chairs of the powerful in this engaging and even funny collection of memories, observations and expert analysis. Interpreting is no easy job, yet the best make it look easy. This is a welcome reminder that beneath the cool exterior of your interpreter's amazingly sweat-free skin is warmth and a human heart.

> **Lane Greene**
> Author of *Talk on the Wild Side*
> Senior Editor at *The Economist*

As a conference interpreter, trainer, and chief interpreter, Ewandro has seen it all. That's what makes this book inspiring and practical. It's full of the down-to-earth information and advice that interpreters, both young and old, need to hear. But most of all, it's just fun to read.

> **Barry Slaughter Olsen**
> Professor of Translation & Interpretation,
> Middlebury Institute of International Studies at Monterey

Warm, honest and relatable: this book reads like Ewandro himself and feels like a chat over coffee. The caring and wise big brother of interpreters has pulled together some of his best tales and thoughts and the result is a book you'll want to take with you on every assignment.

> **Jonathan Downie, Ph.D.**
> Conference Interpreter,
> Author of *Being a Successful Interpreter*

A lifetime of experiences diligently collected and engagingly told. One wishes other senior professionals to keep similar journals for the use of newcomers or those still unsure about the depth of their calling.

> **Franz Baumann, Ph.D.**
> Former United Nations Assistant Secretary-General

CONTENTS

The Door Opens	1
INSPIRATION	
The Power of Language	7
La Vie En Rose	11
Ignorance is Strength	15
Afraid?! Who's Afraid?	21
The Best of The Best	29
The First Man Around the Globe	33
The Accidental Protagonist	37
Interpreter of Maladies	43
Breaking the Starbucks Code	47
No-Sense, No Deal	53
Juggling Two Languages at Once	57
Nice Trumps Nasty	61
How Do You Do That?!	65
INSIGHT	
The Sound of Silence	75
The Compassionate Interpreter	79
Coping Tactics Revisited	85
The Legacy of Jerome	91
The ABC of United Nations	95

Through the Looking Glass	101
Mind Your Language, You @#x!$%*!	105
Biofeedback For Booth Jesters	111
The Fine Art of Blowing It	115
7 Things a Chief Interpreter Wishes You Knew	117

GEAR

Portable Equipment: What to Get and Why	129
Portable Equipment Tips	133
A Cool Portable Equipment Hack	139

TIPS FOR SPEAKERS

What Interpreters Can Tell Speakers About Speaking	143
Speaking Abroad? Here's the Cheat Sheet	149

BIBLIOGRAPHY

Acknowledgments	157
About the Author	159

The Door Opens

Take a good look at this picture. It was taken in Brasilia, Brazil, on Tuesday, March 17, 1992. It shows the precise moment when I became an interpreter.

The gentleman in a light suit is congressman Ibsen Pinheiro. Sitting diagonally from him is His Royal Highness Prince Philip, the Duke of Edinburgh. I am the young guy in the middle. Yup. The one with a lot of hair.

Two weeks later, I was sitting across from the Princess of Thailand and soon after that the Prime

Minister of Norway. In between, a procession of ambassadors came to present their credentials, and they all spoke through me. I had become the personal interpreter to the Speaker of the House, who doubled as Vice-President of the Republic following the impeachment of President Collor.

Four years earlier, I had joined the Lower House of Congress as a clerk and was bored out of my mind pushing papers eight hours a day. Having to wear a suit and tie was another inconvenience. Not long before this I had been a swimming instructor and was accustomed to spending my days with nothing on but a bathing suit and sandals.

The royal entourage was already on its way when the shoe dropped – who would translate for the Duke, who presumably spoke no Portuguese? They realized they would need an interpreter. And with just one hour to go, I was as close as they would ever get to one.

Fishing for a promotion, and perhaps out of overconfidence, I had spread the rumor that I spoke fluent English. And although I could get by, my knowledge was rather patchy, acquired through incomplete courses and random interactions with a handful of friends whose English was just as broken as mine. To my credit, I did a lot of reading in those days, with the help of a few worn-out paper dictionaries.

I was their only shot. At 28 years of age, and with zero interpretation experience under my belt, I was pushed overboard, and I swam.

It took another two years and dozens of consecutive assignments before I would venture into an interpretation booth. It was hard to tell how much progress I was making. But I was having a ball.

Through happenstance —and certainly more mistakes than I was able to acknowledge at the time— I slowly developed into a mature interpreter. That was in the days before the Internet, with little formal training available in Brazil. By necessity, all real learning occurred through trial and error and, whenever possible, through careful observation of more experienced colleagues in the field.

I eventually left my job at the Congress and set up my own translation shop. I would go on to release a book on interpreting and a professional development series for interpreters. I earned a Master's degree in conference interpreting from the Monterey Institute[1] and eventually served as the Chief Interpreter for the International Telecommunication Union, a United Nations agency headquartered in Geneva, Switzerland.

This book is a compilation of musings and stories I have written over my 30 years as a conference interpreter, trainer, manager, and coach. It tells part of my journey. It is an insider's look into an exciting profession that is deeply rooted in history.

If you have ever pictured yourself as an interpreter, chances are you will strongly relate to the challenges one must surmount to penetrate the rather inaccessible world of interpreting. Those tried and tested in the booth will also benefit from the tales and advice shared in the pages that follow, and non-interpreters will hopefully increase their appreciation for languages as they

---

[1] Middlebury Institute of International Studies at Monterey, – www.miis.edu

read these stories.

This is a book about communication at large, and in that sense, it reaches way beyond interpretation, looking inward as well as outward in search of patterns that can make us more effective and mindful communicators.

The articles have been loosely grouped as inspirational and prescriptive, in no particular order. Feel free to read them randomly, jumping ahead and then back as intuition dictates.

The door to the booth has been opened. Come on in. Make yourself comfortable. Put on the headset. Listen to the voices. Contemplate the gestures through the booth window. Let yourself be the interpreter. You will come to see communication in a different light. Using your imagination, you may be surprised to see reflected in the glass a familiar face looking back at you. Maybe you will even hear, above it all, the unmistakable sound of your own voice.

INSPIRATION

The Power of Language

In 1934, an interpreter made history by rendering into French over the radio an important speech given in Nuremberg. Listeners in France were amazed to hear the message in their language just as the words were being pronounced in German. The interpreter was André Kaminker. The speaker, Adolf Hitler. Simultaneous translation had been invented.

A decade later the method was perfected, again in Nuremberg, helping bring closure to the senseless war that Hitler had started. Twenty-one Nazi officials, charged with a variety of offenses and atrocities, were brought to justice in what would go down in history as the first war crimes trial of modern times.

As judges, prosecutors and counselors prepared for the historic Nuremberg Trial, a major practical problem arose. Every testimony and every piece of evidence brought before the court would have to be translated from its original language into another three. Relying on consecutive interpretation —the traditional oral translation technique in which speakers and interpreters take turns— would prove tedious. A new system had to be attempted.

The IBM company had been experimenting with a 'simultaneous telephonic system' and offered its equipment to be pilot-tested at no cost, thereby solving the hardware issue. The challenge of actually making the system work, with instantaneous translations from and into German, English, French, and Russian done by interpreters untrained in the new technique, fell to Leon Dostert, formerly a personal interpreter to General Eisenhower.

The professionals first approached for the job fiercely objected to the proposed system. They resented the impersonality of being placed in an 'aquarium' and the inhuman speed required of them. Dostert, however, insisted that the new system was feasible, and set about to provide whatever minimum training could be given to interpreters, lawyers, and judges in using the new system.

The interpreters recruited were divided into three groups of 12 and relieved one another every 45 minutes. To compensate for the overwhelming mental and psychological effort, they were offered one day off for every two days of work. A most welcome break, after the "never-ending recital of horrors in the courtroom," remembers Patricia Vander Elst, one of the interpreters at Nuremberg. She recalls how stressful it was to live "amidst a sullen native population, in a town that was just a heap of rubble." After just four months in Nuremberg, she says, "I felt ten years older."

Despite their unpreparedness, these pioneers somehow managed to get the job done and even impressed many. Whitney Harris, with the American prosecution staff at Nuremberg, described the translation system in use in these terms:

> *The plan called for an elaborate telephonic installation. From the microphones at the lawyers' lectern, the witness box, and the judges' bench, wires ran to the central interpreters' booth. Whatever was said on an incoming line was instantaneously translated into the other languages by wonderfully skilled interpreters. The interpretations then went into every chair in the courtroom by other telephonic wires, to be picked up through headphones for which a switch was provided to enable the listener to select the preferred language. Flashing red and yellow lights cautioned speakers to become accustomed to it. The instantaneous translation system worked admirably. It was the first time in history that such a system had been used in a judicial proceeding or, for that matter, in any hearing of such length and complexity.*

The trial proceeded for another ten months, setting an important precedent in international law. Of the 21 accused, only three were acquitted. Six were given prison terms, and 13 were sentenced to death by hanging. In his final address to the court, Chief Prosecutor Robert Jackson, from New York, so spoke of the defendants: "They stand before the record of this trial as bloodstained Gloucester stood by the body of his slain king. He begged of the widow, as they beg of you: 'Say I slew them not.' And the Queen replied, 'Then say they were not slain. But dead they are...' "If you were to say of these men that they are not guilty, it would be as true to say that there has been no war, there are no slain, there has been no crime."

Justice Jackson felt that the court had managed to "establish incredible events by credible evidence." He reiterated that the Nazis had been given "a kind of a trial which they, in the days of their pomp and power, never gave any man." Finally, bringing this unprecedented event to a close, as if to reassure the world of the fairness of the proceedings, he said:

"The future will never have to ask, with misgiving, what could the Nazis have said in their favor. History will know that whatever could be said, they were allowed to say."

Indeed, whatever could be said was said and heard in four different languages, thanks to the men and women who dared to challenge conventional wisdom and take a hot seat behind the glass in the far-off year of 1945.

Nuremberg, a city so quintessentially German, had witnessed both the start and end of a vicious war. Like most, it was a war fought with guns and bayonets. And like any other before or since, one triggered and eventually crushed by outstanding speeches. Such is the power of language.

La Vie En Rose

I must have been five or six, but I still remember vividly the day I realized I could read. I was gingerly crossing an intersection in my hometown, my father towing me by the hand, when the hazy neon light in the distance suddenly collapsed into a meaningful string of letters: c-i-n-e-m-a.

The feeling was transcendent. A code had been broken. A veil had been lifted. It felt like I had awakened to another physical sense, one I didn't know existed. All around me words started to come out, shyly and partially at first —RESTAURAN...— then strongly: OPEN, FREE, STOP. They seemed to smile in relief like they had been impatiently waiting to regain their significance after a long, dark night of oblivion.

For a month or so, I sat at my father's battered Remington, punching keys at random in growing frustration at not being able to stitch even one meaningful word together. I was disappointed that the many lines of letters, spaces, and punctuation marks failed to communicate something when I finally whooshed the page out from under the rubbery roll. "Dad, what have I written?" I would ask in hopeful anticipation. "Nothing, son. Nothing really," he would reply, with a benevolent smile that made his eyes squint to a point you would wonder whether he'd gone blind for a moment.

My father would then sit by my side and briefly explain concepts like vowels, consonants and, ultimately, syllables. He would stay just as long as necessary to inspire me to try again. "Oh, I got it, I got it!," I would say impatiently, pushing his hands out of the way to engage in another bout of typing, usually no more effective than the others and just as frustrating. Dad would then retreat until disappointment brought me back, and the process could be repeated. My father knew I had to own the experience and so he would push the door ajar just enough to let some light in, never really swinging it open. Through the crack, albeit narrow, there was no limit to what I could see if I ventured close enough. I guess he wanted me to understand that.

In time, letters stuck into syllables that grew into words and then sentences. And before I knew it, I was standing at that busy intersection in utter amazement. I had pushed the gates with my own hands and stepped into another dimension. It was all magical and exhilarating, of course, but I remember feeling frustrated, too, at being no longer able *not* to read the neon signs. Despite the sudden empowerment, the child in me resented being robbed of its innocence. Colors and shapes had grown into something else. I had grown too and now had to make sense of the world and label my own experiences.

Fast forward ten years. I am now in my teens, trying to learn English. Dad and I are sitting on the floor in the living room with Nat King Cole playing softly in the

The Language Game

background. The song talks of a monkey flying on the back of a buzzard. The images are fun. The language is slangy. *Straighten up and fly right. Cool down, papa, don't you blow your top.* My curiosity is piqued as keywords are translated. Another brave new world is slowly unlocked. Seen through the lenses of language, reality gains a broader, richer perspective.

I am now on my daily commute to Geneva, many years later, listening to a French song on my iPod. The tune is one I have heard a thousand times. Against the backdrop of the snow-capped Alps, the train whizzes past well-trimmed vineyards on the banks of Lake Leman. The Mont Blanc looms into view, and I let my mind wander. I indulge for a second and gradually drift into a silent appreciation of this precious moment. Tilting my head back, I take a deep breath and soak it all in. As I lie there half-awake, marveling at the scenic ride, the lyrics take meaning for the first time. It strikes me hard.

What was once gibberish now resonates in perfectly meaningful French, in a beautiful love song. Another threshold had been crossed into a warm, welcoming universe of opulent mountains, placid waters, and never-ending love. My newly acquired tongue takes me back to my instincts. Colors morph back into feelings rather than words. Through the revolving doors of language, I have come full circle. I am again the kid I once was, standing halfway on that pedestrian crossing. I open my eyes with a jolt, look around and see everything anew.

Edith Piaf had been telling me all along: through the lenses of love and bliss, life takes on beautiful rosy hues. I can see clearly now. My innocence is restored. I smile wide and squint my eyes so hard you'd think me blind for a moment. Yet through that crack, albeit narrow, for the first time in years… *je vois la vie en rose.*

Ignorance is Strength

In 1988, I was living in Konstanz, Germany, as a graduate student. The Seoul Olympics were upon us. I would compromise on anything, as long as I didn't miss the men's 100-meter dash final, the long-awaited confrontation between the legendary Carl Lewis and the Jamaican turned Canadian Ben Johnson.

The TV set in my dorm room had been found on the street, two days prior, in a popular German exchange tradition called *Spermüll*. It was a battered, black and white 15-inch, and much to my surprise, it worked fine.

Just for half an hour, though. At the end of 30 minutes, the circuitry heated up, and the image got fuzzy. A few seconds more and it all spiraled into an indistinct vortex, with the sound soon going, too. At that point, my TV had to be turned off and left to cool for another half an hour.

In time I devised an ingenious way to keep abreast of the news and follow at least the Formula 1 races. I would switch the TV on and off at timed 30-minute intervals. With the help of precisely-timed German TV airings, I did just fine.

But in the 100-meter Olympic final, it all went south, and there was no telling when the race would start. I prayed that my 30-minute allowance would hold long enough. It didn't. The athletes were barely off their starting blocks when the race tracks all merged in an indecipherable, soundless contrail. I spent the rest of the night, several time zones away, desperately turning the clunky channel knob for 30 minutes at a time, to no avail.

Back in the day, a sprinter's reaction time —i.e., how fast the racer reacts to the firing of the gun— was believed to be a genetic trait. Ben Johnson was naturally gifted in that regard and spring-loaded ahead of all others. But I could bet all my chips that Carl Lewis would eventually recover the lost terrain and overtake the Canadian, who looked too bulky to be fast.

In high-performance sports, success is a somewhat predictable business. A simple test of an athlete's muscle fibers will indicate the disciplines at which he or she will excel. Champions are cherry-picked early on, in a process that involves popularization and careful screening.

Uncooking the soup

When I later transitioned from fitness to interpreting, I thought it only natural that the same logic would apply. I tended to believe that the great interpreters were born and privileged by a fully multilingual upbringing, with two or more languages occurring naturally and effortlessly. In my mind, a top-notch interpreter would necessarily have been born in a fully bilingual environment. Success required absolute mastery of all one's working languages without a trace of an accent. The ability to interpret simultaneously was, just like the sprinter's reaction time, a genetically encoded, unalterable attribute. Or so I thought.

My subsequent career as a trainer of interpreters would soon disprove the thesis. As it soon became evident, the notion that interpreting results from innate talent is just the first of a series of misconceptions about the trade. In a training environment, candidates with perfect linguistic credentials have the hardest time getting past the initial exercises. While they rely on a vocabulary that is far more complete than that of their peers, they tend to be too demanding on themselves and come to expect a level of performance that is simply unattainable when you're just starting out. Their frustration mounts when the next classmate in the booth does surprisingly well, despite her limitations.

Humans are competitive by nature, but our self-knowledge is always limited. The better our skills, and the awareness of such skills, the higher our self-imposed demands. Upon realizing one's comparative edge —say, one's fully bilingual abilities— it is easy to feel overwhelmed by the weight of responsibility. With that responsibility comes fear and performance suffers.

But there is more to it. An interesting process goes on inside the fully bilingual mind. In time, different languages and cultural experiences blend into one another in a seamless flow. The many semantic constructs, and the different rational and emotional responses elicited by each, eventually fuse into one same melting pot of common experiences, one single database. In a fully bilingual mind, what we would call 'translation' occurs naturally, in an unconscious exercise that will later make it all seem artificial when one has to interpret and look for equivalences.

Now, for those of us who learned a foreign language through conscious effort, there will always be the perception of two distinct worlds. While they touch one another, they never fully intersect. Communication then becomes an accumulation of linguistic and metalinguistic mechanisms, with much attention given to gestures and subtle intonation changes. This creates the need for alternative communication tactics, and it imposes greater reliance on ancillary inputs such as body language. With the right personality and hard work, such a process, although equally unconscious, may work to one's advantage in the interpretation booth.

On the surface, this analysis may seem obvious or common sense, but it lends itself to rather intriguing inferences. Our way of thinking, our emotional reactions, our language, our inflexibility, our ability to improvise, our informality and casualness are, in no small part, defined by the cultures in which we grew up. And the way in which we acquire our languages will largely determine the functioning of our mind, our predispositions, our prejudices, our outlook on the world, our personality, even. The frontier between language and cognition is still fuzzy, with little consensus so far as to what comes first — speech or thought. The shape of our hands and our dexterity differentiated us from other primates, gradually allowing us tactile and manipulative experiences that would eventually create new synaptic pathways and ultimately enhance our cognitive potential. Analogously, our speech and the virtues or limitations of our languages configure and discipline our way of thinking and how we look upon the world.

For most of us, white is a distinct color, or the plain absence thereof, the opposite of black. For an Inuit, white is a continuum of multiple shades, each carrying a specific label and triggering a linguistic and emotional reaction of its own. What for us is just a bland semantic attribute, a flat adjective, to an Inuit requires the mastery of a far vaster vocabulary, with sensorial and logical implications that are *literally* visible.

Language acquisition is an individualized process with a collective counterpoint where our choices are validated or refuted by our environment and labeled success or failure depending on how high they score vis-à-vis a shared repository of cultural references. These references, in turn, transcend the mere linguistic realm, though. Caucasians usually think of a zebra as a white animal with black stripes, but a native African may see it as a white-striped black horse. A person born and raised in the United States will readily understand the practicality of killing two birds with one stone. But a Brazilian like me will likely picture two rabbits being struck dead by a single blow of a club.

These choices tend to occur naturally, without much conscious elaboration. For interpreters or translators, irrespective of our bilingualism, several of these conceptual and linguistic cross-references need to be deconstructed. A different process is set in motion, forcing us to trace back our steps and undo associations made long ago. We feel the need to see the world through two distinct sets of lenses which, in the case of bilinguals, had merged long ago. In a certain way, we need to unlearn.

The situation can't help but bring to mind Winston Smith, the main character in *1984*, overwhelmed by the cruelty of a world where truth and lie were relative concepts and where "stupidity was as necessary as intelligence and as difficult to attain." Paradoxically, in interpretation, as in the surreal world of Orwell, ignorance is strength, too.

It is great to rely on some competitive advantage —a superior reaction time if you're a sprinter, or a prodigious memory if you're an interpreter. But to keep ahead of the curve and sustain your lead without any fear of the post-race blood screening, one needs more than just a head start.

Over the edge

The morning after my sleepless night at that university dorm in Konstanz, the *Südkurier* pictured the Canadian crossing the finish line ahead of all others, his arm provocatively raised in victory while still in motion. New world record: 9:79s.

As the saying goes, success comes before work only in dictionaries (for most languages, at least). Our competitive edge, whatever it is, will carry us only halfway. The home stretch to the imaginary finish line requires much sweat and dedication.

To everyone's dismay, Johnson tested positive for performance-enhancing drugs following the race. Despite his competitive advantage, his success was short-lived. He had to surrender his medal to his rival and was banned from sports for good. The flying Canadian, the Big Ben as they used to call him, the second-best sprinter in the world was turned off and left to cool.

Just like my cheap TV set.

Afraid?! Who's Afraid?

Taking a new step, uttering a new word, is what people fear most.

— F. Dostoyevski

In my early days as a linguist, consecutive interpretation was all I did and all I was comfortable doing. It all changed one morning.

I showed up for what I thought was going to be business as usual and proceeded to greet the speaker I would be interpreting. We shook hands and engaged in casual chat, slowly drifting towards the back of the auditorium as we spoke. Before I knew it, I was standing by the door of a fully equipped interpretation booth.

"We'll start as soon as you're ready," she said, pointing to the chair in the little cubicle. I contemplated it for a second, somewhat puzzled, and tried to clear up the obvious misunderstanding. At the end of a series of indistinct expressions of denial on my part, she cut me short, glancing at her watch and looking hurried: "You'll be fine."

I can still recall the anxiety. It was not new. But the last time I had felt anything close, I was being pushed out of an airplane mid-flight, with an awkward backpack tied around my torso. I let my body fall off into thin air for about five seconds and was relieved when the knapsack unbolt into a huge, green umbrella letting me glide smoothly over beautiful meadows, trees, and houses just out of town.

Once the parachute opens, it is easy to feel empowered. But at the door of that noisy single-engine airplane two thousand feet off the ground, there are no heroes. Not among first-timers, at least. After a month of intensive training, I had learned how to fold meters of cords and fabric and squeeze the fat bundle into a bag that would hardly accommodate a pillow. I was ready for my first jump. And, of course, I was petrified.

As the plane soared, so did my fear. At that point, you just sit there and try your best to look tough and not panic, all along wondering how you are going to respond when it is your turn to jump off. Luckily, there is always a 'friend' to help you through this fleeting moment of indecision. You don't jump. You're pushed out. But once back on the ground, you feel you're the bravest guy alive.

I wish I could say I felt as brave that first day in the booth, but that would be twisting the truth a little. Before I could voice any objection, the speaker was gone. The lights went off, and the audience plunged into the deepest of silences. The plane was off the ground, and the push had come in the form of a clear-cut command in English: "Get in there and do the best you can." I sat down and put on the clunky earphones. I had jumped and now felt sucked full speed towards the bottom of a vertiginous cliff.

Free fall

The Language Game

Fear is a powerful emotion. Within reasonable limits, it is a healthy disposition that protects and preserves us. Yet phobic fear is not just unhealthy but incapacitating. Jack it up a notch and you're in panic mode, deprived of your ability to think. That's when the rational mind abandons the boat and leaves at the helm the proto-brain we inherited from some distant cousins in the evolutionary trail, an encephalon capable of nothing but basic instincts of reproduction and life preservation.

Under intense fear, we slide back as a species. We revert to mere primates. We fear simply, without the slightest clue as to the origin of our fears, most of which unfounded. Under extreme circumstances, without the counterpoint of reason, a series of overlapping irrational worries start to pile up, eventually triggering a physiological chain reaction in response to actual or imaginary threats. This process may quickly escalate to a surge beyond control.

Interpreters are no strangers to fear. Budding interpreters, in particular, are very fear-prone. They place themselves under unrealistic expectations. They tell themselves they mustn't fail or draw a blank, lest their career will come to an end before it even starts. They panic at the judgment of others and are quick to engage in negative self-talk that may rapidly spiral out of control. In their semi-paranoid fantasy, Murphy's Law becomes as ubiquitous as the Law of Gravity and equally unforgiving the minute they set foot in the booth.

As beginners, our fears are mostly circumstantial. They stem from the uncertainty surrounding a craft one doesn't quite yet know. They are also self-centered, by and large. Sure, you must get it right and deliver a flawless interpretation, but take an honest, deep look at your fears and you'll probably admit that you are not that worried that the message may eventually get twisted for those in the audience. Your stress level doesn't yet afford such an ethical sophistication. Having your shortcomings exposed is what scares you.

Now, if you are a novice interpreter and you feel like you are not afraid of anything, mind the words of Greek philosopher Thucydides: "Ignorance is bold." Worry not. As you progress in your career, your fear of failure will gradually be replaced with genuine sympathy for your audience. At some point, the true measure of your responsibility, a different kind of concern, will start to weigh on your shoulders. This apprehension is positive and comes with experience. It breeds, rather than undermine confidence.

Cruising

Contrary to popular belief, the biggest limiting factor in conference interpretation is not linguistic. It is emotional. Mastery of the most challenging vocabulary will be of little use in the absence of the fine stress management skills required to talk your way out of trouble. The possibility of failure dramatically increases when you're in panic mode. Actions geared at taming your anxiety should, therefore, be assigned the highest priority.

Escaping the stronghold of your fears involves confrontation and exposure. To progress beyond fear, you must face it. You must project outward and put yourself to the test until you can draw the line that will allow you to choose between flight and fight every time. Pressing through and beyond your fears takes determination and resolve. It is a *yang* approach, the disciplined way. As Michel de Montaigne once said, "it takes courage to be afraid."

Courage is the disposition to face our demons at a time when we feel weakest, without a clue as to our real chances of success. Courage is the deliberate decision to run some serious risks and bear the consequences, from the realization that not doing so may eventually harm us more. However, confrontation alone doesn't free us from fear. Courage should not be just a call to war. It should also be an invitation to reconcile rather than subjugate our ego. In our quest to conquer fear, a softer, *yin* approach is equally important and far more effective.

Adjusting your expectations is a good first step. Next time if you feel anxious, try challenging some of your beliefs and altering your perspective. First off, imagining that the audience has attended the meeting just to appreciate or critique your performance as an interpreter is an unnecessary exercise in vanity. Nobody is there for you. Interpreters play a vital role, but just as well a support role. For the most part, people will be oblivious of you. Moreover, whatever fleeting thought they might spare for that poor soul in the booth will probably be a reassuring one. They are not out to get you, and they don't *impose* their expectations on you. They genuinely *want* you to succeed and will forge an alliance with you early on, if you let them. This should help abate your fear a bit.

Next, train yourself to go beyond fighting or resisting your anxiety. Remind yourself of the true reason why you are there and gently shift the focus away from you. Put the audience first and silently reiterate your commitment to serve them in the best possible way. Ultimately, the antidote for fear is not brute force, but love. Learn to love, rather than dread, your professional insecurities. Honor your courage in stepping up to the plate despite your shortcomings, for the benefit of others.

Then sit back, relax and get out of everybody's way, including yourself. Problems and accidents can happen to anyone, but between possibility and probability, there is an immense field. That is where you want to be. Admit the possibility, but live in the probability. There are no assurances in life, but you are free to choose that in which you *prefer* to believe.

Safe landing

The use of interpreters dates back to time immemorial and will probably linger for many centuries more until humankind speaks one single language (or Google comes up with an iPhone app for instant interpretation, whatever happens first). Until the day comes, we need to discharge our professional functions conscientiously and responsibly.

Do not underestimate the circumstances. Do not overestimate your gear or your skills. Gently fold and verify every cord and square inch of your parachute before a jump. Rehearse your actions and be sure to carry a reserve canopy. Never underrate the importance or complexity of a speech. Be diligent in your search for information on the talk and the speaker. Prepare your glossaries. Anticipate pitfalls. Have a plan B. Get the right training and sharpen your tools regularly. Then, and only then, do the desensitizing drills suggested here. Only then board a plane or enter a booth, with or without fear. You may survive your first couple of experiences out of sheer luck as I have. However, to do it consistently, you'll need to get serious about your passion or profession. A newly-acquired ability to control your emotions is no excuse not to prepare.

The Language Game

The three jumps I had so far logged in my promising career as a skydiver had done a lot for my self-confidence, but a frustrated, nearly-tragic fourth dive buried my dreams of Icarus forever. The dual-engine Navajo darted through the dirt runway of the battered airfield in the outskirts of Brasilia. It had barely taken off the ground when it bumped across and struck dead a stray horse. In true rodeo style, the captain managed to jolt the aircraft down to firm land and slowly taxied us back to safety, despite the copious fuel leakage we could see and smell through the plane's open door.

Back at the impromptu terminal, we quickly deplaned on very shaky legs and a sick stomach. I laid my gear on the ground one last time, walked away from the aircraft and never turned back. It was about 7 pm, and darkness had fallen. We knew we had exceeded the take-off deadline by at least one hour. My recently acquired confidence was fast turning into neglect, and the experience I had just survived was a benign wake-up call.

May the near-disastrous end of my flying career be an equally gentle reminder to you, as well. An unexpected or early failure in the booth may prove just as off-putting. Shoot happens. When it does, you'll want to be ready.

Expect the best, but be ready for the worst. Keep cool but vigilant and remember the skydiving adage: "There are old jumpers, and there are bold jumpers, but there are no old, bold jumpers." All it takes for things to go south is one entangled cord, a minute tear on your gear or a stray horse crossing your way.

The Best of The Best

"Welcome to the largest multilingual summit this office has ever organized. Congratulations on making it here. You are the best of the best."

With these words, the chief interpreter of a top international organization greeted the 70 or so interpreters who gathered around the u-shaped table for the pre-event briefing in Washington, DC. Half of the group had heard similar praise before and took it for what it was. The rookies among us received the compliment sheepishly, trying hard to act matter-of-factly while secretly wishing their mothers had been there.

Ours is a funny business. As interpreters, we tend to get rated in relation to someone other than us—and whose prestige we hope will rub off on us for a brief moment in time. It's not uncommon to refer to a colleague as 'the interpreter of President Such and Such,' or to elevate someone instantly by saying 'she interpreted for _____'" (fill in the blank: Madonna, the Pope, Obama). No word seems to be needed regarding how well she performed at the job. The distinction of having been picked for such a salient assignment seems to suffice as a tag of success.

Now, while we all occasionally play the celebrity

card and name-dropping to our advantage—as we well should—anyone who has been in this business long enough understands that true success in our line of work lies somewhere else, usually a few notches down the superstar scale.

Chief interpreters are aware of the power of applause and criticism and will dispense them accordingly, on an as-needed basis. And while preemptive praise can go a long way for team building or as a confidence booster, it more often than not aims at imparting a sense of responsibility rather than importance. At its core, stripped of the heightened sense of self it is designed to trigger, the message means, simply: "Please, don't screw this up."

Now, are you truly the best interpreter out there? In the absence of a true benchmark against which to gauge your progress, how can you tell if you've made it? Before you start racking your brain for answers, here is another question you may want to ponder along with the rest: does it matter?

As freelancers at the mercy of market conditions, we compete against one another for a dwindling number of contracts. Hitting a few home runs, while a great achievement, is not a reliable long-term measure of success, especially if flashy assignments are few and far between. There is nothing wrong in enjoying the exposure such high-level assignments provide, and you should, by all means, capitalize on them as openly as you ethically can. But at the end of the day, success is not determined by how royal the ball or how tall the celebrity in whose shadow we stand. In fact, who hires us matters less than the fact that they do or how often they do.

Also, past success is said to breed failure if you indulge in it too soon, while tomorrow still needs to be filled with work. In a career as long as ours, stamina beats speed. We're all in it for the long haul. Consistency rules. If you want to know how successful you truly are, look at your calendar.

But the question still begs an answer. Have you made it? On a good day, we all like to think we have. We're still around, after all, with a growing track record behind us and the promise of greener pastures ahead. As for bad days, of which there will be a few, you can always dust off that picture of you and _____ (fill in the blank).

The First Man Around the Globe

Most people think of Ferdinand Magellan as the Portuguese explorer who first sailed around the planet on a quest to prove that the Earth was round. Now, consider this.

While Magellan did sail from Spain on an expedition that eventually went full circle, he never completed the tour. Also, Magellan never set out to sail around the globe. His goal was to establish a western route to the spices that grew in the Indies. Used as seasonings, food preservatives, and aphrodisiacs, these exotic commodities were worth many times their weight in gold. With as little as a sack of cloves, one could buy a house, settle down on a good pension, and never leave port again.

Assuming the Earth to be round, Magellan was confident he could find the fabled maritime passage through the continents that had been claimed earlier by Portugal and Spain, the two competing seafaring superpowers of the time.

A few decades earlier, under pressure from the catholic rulers of Spain, the Pope had drawn an imaginary line on the map from pole to pole and divided the world in two. Spain was granted exclusive rights to territories west of the divide, with Portugal expected to keep to the east.

The deal was sealed in the small Spanish town of Tordesillas.

Dismissed by King Manuel of Portugal, to whom he first pitched the idea of an expedition, a humiliated Magellan crossed the border into Spain where he got the attention of King Charles I, then in his teens. When Magellan authoritatively declared that the Spice Islands lay in the Spanish hemisphere and that he knew how to get there, the Spanish monarch was sold.

On September 20, 1519, five ships carrying 260 men headed into the unknown. Sailing southwest, the armada made a pleasant landfall in the tropics. As they proceeded south, any waterway leading inland was explored in search of the canal.

The Spaniards resented having a Portuguese at the helm. As the weather worsened and provisions dwindled, their impatience escalated into full-blown mutiny, which Magellan crushed with unspeakable cruelty. Mutineers were marooned, eviscerated alive or dismembered, their heads and limbs displayed on the five ships as a warning.

Sour at the captain's brutality, the crew of the *San Antonio* defected back to Spain, carrying with it most of the provisions. And during a reconnaissance journey, the *Santiago* ran aground.

On November 1, Magellan started exploring a westward navigable seaway. Twenty-seven freezing days later the three remaining ships emerged into the *Mar Pacifico*. The legendary strait connecting east and west had been found and crossed.

Past the strait, it would take the crew 98 days to see dry land again. Scurvy and famine claimed the lives of dozens of seamen. After replenishments and repairs in modern-day Guam, the fleet advanced into what would later be the Philippines. To everyone's surprise, Magellan's slave Henry, acquired in a journey to Malacca eight years earlier and brought along as an interpreter, could easily communicate with the rulers and natives in the various islands, which Magellan claimed for Spain.

With Henry's linguistic support and the imposing thunder of canons, Magellan had no trouble claiming a few islands for Spain. But when he tried to convert chieftain Lapu Lapu to Christianity by force, his fate was sealed on the island of Mactan. Shallow waters kept the ships away and cannon shots out of range. Overconfident and severely outnumbered, Magellan was killed brutally, along with another eight Europeans.

With his master dead, Henry was free. Furthermore, he found himself back *home*. If Henry was actually from the Cebu region—as his command of the local language indicates—the first man to circumnavigate the world was actually an interpreter.

But the expedition still had to navigate the maze of islands on its way back to Spain, and the new captains refused to release the interpreter. Disgruntled, Henry turned to Rajah Humabon, the ruler of Cebu, and plotted a conspiracy. He convinced the King to offer a farewell banquet to about 30 Europeans. As the feast came to a close, archers emerged from the bushes and killed all the guests but one: Henry.

After this, the Spaniards burned one of their ships and proceeded to the Spice Islands. Having also lost the *Trinidad*, they resorted to raiding passing ships and eventually reached the spices with a new interpreter: Antonio Pigafetta.

An Italian scholar and explorer from Venice,

Pigafetta kept a detailed journal of the expedition's activities. He also compiled the first phrasebook in history with the help of Henry. Filled with drawings, Pigafetta's journal provides a rich guide to the features and customs of the lands and peoples encountered during the voyage.

Finally, on September 10, 1522, a battered ship docked at the port of Seville, manned by a skeleton crew of just 18 sailors. They were severely malnourished. Most could hardly walk. Despite the hardships, the *Victoria*, and what was left of its crew, had changed the world forever. And what little cargo it held was enough to turn a profit.

Despite his early death, Magellan earned his place in history. He had galaxies and space programs named after him. Sebastián Elcano, the pilot who rounded the Cape of Good Hope and steered the *Victoria* back home, was also celebrated in Spain with a coat of arms and his face on currency bills and stamps.

But to be fair, their glory would have to be shared with at least another two crew members. First, Pigafetta, without whom most of the story would have perished along with the ships. And finally Henry, the expedition's interpreter, who made communication possible and who arguably went full circle earlier than anyone else.

Coming from opposite ends of the social spectrum, the Venetian nobleman and the humble slave accidentally brought on board weapons many times more persuasive than the sword to change history: their pen and their voice.

The Accidental Protagonist

Endearing, controversial, genuine or stereotypically mean, a relatable character is key in any plot.

It helps if the protagonist's life is eventful and glamorous, or if her job is somehow awe-inspiring or tinged with a hint of mystery. Add a drop of mischief and intrigue, some eavesdropping and world-changing encounters, and the magical spell is cast.

Perhaps partially for that reason, a growing number of works in literary and cinematic fiction that have recently hit the big screen and bookstore shelves revolve around conference interpreters. Interpreters seem to have a spellbinding effect on people.

From a distance, it all looks like magic. Up close, it looks like madness. Two people sitting behind a glass pane in a dimly lit cubicle, listening and speaking at the same time, repeating in a different language words and ideas that are not their own.

They have no control over the complexity, the speed, the clarity, or the logic of the original presentation. They must link their own segments of speech together, mindful of any sentences left dangling, as they strive to correctly close a parenthetical remark opened by the speaker in the subjunctive tense, and then pick up where she left off. They must maintain a speechless side conversation with their booth mate by way of meaningful looks, gestures, and notes. They may also have to read through a document or look up words in a glossary while they are talking, sometimes delaying the interpretation until the full picture can be formed in their mind.

As if that weren't enough, interpreters are usually at the opposite end of the conference room from the speaker, away from view and unable to slow her down or stop her for clarification. They are not exactly present in the room, but their omnipresent voices are just a click away. It makes you wonder.

This perplexity at one's apparently magical ability to hear speech in one language and render it orally into another, in real-time, is akin to the fascination people experience when watching an illusionist's show. You know a trick is being performed, you just don't know exactly how. Eventually, you agree to temporarily suspend your disbelief and give in to the fantasy, lest the thrill should fade away.

In time, conference-goers get a handle on the mechanics and training that make it all possible, and the amazement gradually wears off. At that point, their curiosity, once confined to practical and linguistic aspects, slowly gives way to a different type of speculation surrounding the true identity of the men and women behind those evanescent, faceless voices. That secondary fascination has gained traction with a much broader audience in recent years, as more writers and playwrights explore the peculiarities of these linguistic mediators.

Most of the works employ the cloak and dagger approach. Take the example of Sidney Pollack's *The*

The Language Game

Interpreter, which was not only a box office hit but was the first to be filmed at the UN headquarters in New York, a privilege previously denied to Alfred Hitchcock.

In this highly suspenseful film, the protagonist, played by Nicole Kidman, is a United Nations interpreter who inadvertently eavesdrops on a plan to assassinate the odious dictator of her imaginary African country. Before long, she becomes the target of the very conspiracy she accidentally uncovers, and spends the rest of the film running for her life—or making out with the cop assigned to protect her (sure, a little love never hurts).

Slightly more realistic and specific, but still in the realm of fiction, is the book by Kim Suki, also called *The Interpreter*. Suki's novel centers on the life of a young Korean interpreter who uses her work to unearth details of her own upbringing. Here the investigation turns inward, in more of a psychological thriller. And in a third book sharing that same title, Suzanne Glass—who was once a conference interpreter—explores the ethical issue of professional secrecy, exposing the drama of Dominique, who learns of a plan to conceal a possible cure for AIDS while interpreting at an international conference. More espionage and mystery.

Another novel, *The Mission Song*, by Britain's John le Carré, features Bruno Salvador, Salvo for short, a competent interpreter of African languages, including Swahili. In a book filled with interesting insights about interpreting and the nature of languages, le Carré graces us with yet another thriller.

Rounding out the action-packed circuit of political intrigue is *Bel Canto*, by American novelist—and former opera singer—Ann Patchett. Modeled on the Japanese embassy hostage crisis in Lima, a group of jet-setters and diplomats gathered for a private opera performance find themselves besieged by terrorists bent on killing the president of an unnamed South American country.

Once the captors realize the president is not in attendance, hours of negotiation and bonding ensue, led by Gen Watanabe, the personal interpreter for a visiting Japanese mogul, who rather conveniently seems to master every language being used in the room, including the terrorists'. The bad guys end up dead, as does Gen's boss. The interpreter saves the day and gets to marry the opera star. Sorry to have spoiled it for you.

But perhaps the most interesting work of fiction to indirectly address the work of interpreters breaks away from the espionage genre. It is, rather, a love story. According to the author, Nobel-laureate Mario Vargas Llosa, it is a modern romance, as symbiotic and neurotic as the world is today and closer to reality than the stereotypical literary romantic love.

It tells the adventures and misfortunes of Ricardo Somocurcio, a Peruvian who pursues the woman he loves over four decades on three continents. *The Bad Girl* avoids the cliché that has interpreters cruising the world as international negotiators, rubbing shoulders with the rich and famous.

No more covert meetings in London, New York, and Davos. Forget the occasional world-saving incursions into wild African hamlets and exotic Asian destinations. Llosa's interpreter is a rather simple, undecided, almost naïve man. Not the type one would expect to weigh in on negotiations that could seal the fate of the planet. He'd be lucky to sort out his own love life.

Ricardo does travel the world and lives in Paris as a staff interpreter for Unesco. But that is as far as the stereotypes go. His lover, a textbook sociopath—with all the endearing charm that entails—pushes him around and leads him by the nose while exhibiting shameless derision for interpreting, which she often dismisses as that "profession of phantoms."

In the words of Lily, the novel's gold-digging *femme fatale*, Ricardo is "nothing but an interpreter (...) someone who *is* only when he isn't, a hominid who exists when he stops being what he is so that what other people think and say can pass through him more easily."

Vargas Llosa, a globetrotting writer who once doubled as a politician and presidential hopeful in his native Peru, has undoubtedly been exposed to interpreters countless times in the course of his career, despite his mastery of Spanish, French, and English. That allows him to cut through the cliché with critical reflections on the impersonal and at times frustrating nature of an interpreter's job. The result is a relatable, if wimpy, main character one can root for.

In a progression that is typical of many first- and second-generation interpreters, Ricardo starts his career as a translator and gradually teaches himself interpreting, thus adding another few notches to his belt.

He proceeds in fits and starts, facing enormous difficulties in landing his first gigs as an interpreter, in a professional circle that is a lot tighter than that of translators, and where the professional associations "admit new members sparingly."

A tale of thwarted passion, *The Bad Girl,* also offers a good overview of the social and political transformations that have taken place in Europe and, above all, in Latin America in recent years, as seen through the creative eyes of Vargas Llosa, one of its real-life protagonists. All of it served up with a certain lyrical detachment, right touches of humor, and the bitter reminiscences of someone who realizes he may not remember any of the millions of words he has had to translate, "because not a single one deserved to be remembered."

This article was not intended as a book review, but Llosa's rich and agreeable prose is worth praising if anything for avoiding the stereotypes and easy suspense formula. And, while dwelling on some of the less flattering nuances of an interpreter's craft, and on the silly mistakes we all make when in love, his realistic assessment of what defines us as interpreters or lovers is, again, refreshing, in a society where sugarcoating and instant celebrities have sadly become the norm.

Interpreter of Maladies

I am ushered through a backdoor by a Korean who calls himself Francisco and who happens to speak near-perfect English, Spanish, and Portuguese. He is a regular and quickly shows me around. I sign myself in and stand at a busy intersection of narrow corridors, on occasion leaning out of the way to dodge a nurse or wheelchair.

The first patient approaches, followed by the doctor. I close the door behind me once the three of us have enter the small office. Pablo begins: back pain, difficulty getting out of bed, hard time walking. Complaints overlap as profusely as Spanish words permit, with the patient doing his best to squeeze all his acute and chronic symptoms into the long-awaited five-minute visit. I give his maladies and discomfort a varnish of English as I carry them over to the doctor's end of the table. Free prescription drugs and recommendations travel back through me in Spanish disguise, landing soothingly on Pablo's ears. He'll be OK soon. No big deal. "Gracias, gracias."

It's now Maria, Spanish-speaking, Mexican-looking, though actually from Central America. Sad expression, rude hands, voice almost inaudible at the end of a long day of work. Skyrocketing blood pressure, abundant palpitations. "My legs itch and burn when I open the fridge" - go figure! Eleven years in the United States, no English. Homesick and yet unwilling to go back. She needs hypertension medication. She needs a well-deserved rest she cannot afford. She needs attention as well but is probably too shy to make it known.

I do my bridging number as I best can, imbuing my rendering with empathy and respect, yet careful not to side with either party. Minutes fly by, and the narrow time slot is soon over. Maria pushes herself down from the table with a sigh, her chest probably a notch lighter. She almost smiles as she and her doctor shake hands. "Que te vaya bien!" Now it is the doctor who smiles in gratitude.

I allow myself a candy while my colleagues see other pablos and marias in adjacent rooms, in a free health clinic for low-income people, the only hope available to many an immigrant and worker in a 50-mile radius. We're volunteers helping an English-speaking medical staff communicate in Spanish. Quite a change of gears for conference interpreters like us. Back to consecutive, one-on-one interpretation, in close human interaction. We have emerged from behind the scenes for a close-up look at things in a world of personal, pressing needs.

In-booth conference interpretation, though mostly exhilarating, can be sterile at times. You see the world from a dimly lit cubicle separated from everything else by a solid glass pane, your emotions firewalled by a sophisticated set of gadgets. You are a faceless and evanescent intruder, soon forgotten after the session is adjourned. No lasting impression is left. No permanent memory lingers. No genuine engagement to speak of. You see the world as if through a long telescope, and the only part of you piercing through is that metallic voice.

The Language Game

Not at the clinic, though. Here one can't help rubbing shoulders with reality. Here you commit your every sense. Interpreters gain a distinct face, and so do people. Patients have a name, and so do you. Doctors are suddenly too big to hide behind their coats. You stand close enough to hear them breathe. You feel the voices tremble as intimate details are revealed. You watch their gaze scrutinize the floor for signs of hope and away from fear. You shake the hands of ordinary people who long to rest their weary heads on human shoulders, albeit foreign.

Healthcare interpretation is a gentle reminder of what interpreting is about: humans interacting to satisfy immediate needs. It is a departure from the dull routine of stale salutes and compliments lacquered in studied urbanity. It's an invitation to push ajar the doors of our booths and our soul for a healing gust of fresh air.

Breaking the Starbucks Code

I am an unusual Brazilian, for I hate coffee. Well, I don't particularly hate it, but for the most part, I don't remember it exists. Until a friend buys me some, that is. I then will sit and sip it slowly enough to get me through a conversation without embarrassing my host. Half of my cup will be cream, anyway. And sugar. Lots of it (these days the yellow stuff, actually). Yes, I like my coffee sweet.

For most Brazilians, myself included, coffee is an integral part of civilized life. To be offered some is a welcome sign of appreciation, the opportunity for a well-deserved break, an invitation to chit-chat or a chance to close a deal. So, I never push the cup away, although I hate it. Then again, it's just coffee. Boiling water put through some roasted ground beans. The options on how to have it done vary from strong to mild and from sweet to black. Period. There is not much else to it. All Brazilians (and I bet even Colombians) would agree there *should not* be much more to it. Unless, of course, you are in America.

America is a different ball game. And the ball game is called Starbucks. I used to go there a lot, usually to accompany my wife, who suffers from a severe case of coffee addiction. I have learned that depriving her of coffee is not the safest thing to do, and so I usually settle for some decaf. But I never get it right. Have not at least, so far. Not once.

Starbucks is as much a pleasant gourmet experience as it is an unpleasant language nightmare. Even for the coffee-savvy. Their communication strategy seems purposefully designed to mix you up, and most of the servers behind the counter speak a language other than English, which then again is never my own. At Starbucks, one is left to wonder how coffee can possibly present in so many varieties and proceed from (allegedly) so many different sites. There is, for example, the Brazil Ipanema Bourbon, which of course is unheard of in Brazil —or in Ipanema, for that matter. You can also have the Joya del Día or the Ubora blend, and then Sumatra, Costa Rica, Guatemala and a list of countries as long as the UN roster.

Once you have decided where you would like your taste buds to travel, you find yourself under pressure to nod or shake your head through a series of further yes-or-no questions: Strong roast? Venti or tall? Grande, maybe? Whipped cream? For here or to go? Not getting half of these queries, and too embarrassed to keep an angry line waiting through a tedious menu repetition, I rake my mind for quick ways out of that conundrum. I have tried many different strategies and abandoned just as many. Checking the giant menu board hanging from the ceiling does not work, trust me. Their signage, which should help you order quickly and comfortably, does the exact opposite. Starbucks uses a language of its own. Here *tall* means small, and *grande* —which is *large* in Spanish— means medium. The only option left as the probable opposite of small is *venti*, which is Italian for *twenty*. Now, why twenty? Why not *mille ('thousand', if we are sticking with Italian)* or *fifty*? And what's with *tall*? What about *short*? —or its equivalent in Spanish: *corto*.

The Language Game

At the end of about 15 seconds of awkward silence, I choose to try my luck as the questions are repeated. I alternate between 'yes', 'no' and random pointing, all the way through 'next customer, please'. I then sit in resignation, waiting to see what the heck I have ordered this time, knowing fully well that I still have one challenge ahead: recognizing my order when the barista shouts it at the far end of the counter, always badly butchering my name: "a grande pumpkin latte mocha frappuccino to go for Mr. Magorrailles." Well, I guess that would be me!

Coffee in hand, I let my mind wander, as I try to regain my balance. There must be a secret code here somewhere, and the Robert Langdon in me is determined to break it. The initial evidence is telling. It is not unusual for ciphers to combine different languages following a logic known only to codebreakers. As in every code, the idea is to reveal some covert intention or plan, while on the surface keeping the explicit message totally inconspicuous. Perhaps the letters in 'Ipanema' reveal a secret plot if one shuffles them right. Maybe the mention to those pleasure-inspiring tourist destinations are geographic coordinates in disguise. I mean, why else would they be there? Do I really care what coffee tastes like in Sumatra?

Then again given that the underlying premise shared by any language code is the effort not to make sense —at least not explicitly— you would expect a business like Starbucks to rely on something else to keep pouring the ridiculous amount of coffee it does on a typical day at its many shops throughout the world. Yet the code, cryptic or subliminal as it may be, seems to be working well for the company. It keeps customers on their toes, guessing in endless trial and error and coming back for more until they have tasted the entire menu. How else could they tell a *frappuccino* from *cappuccino*, a *chai* from a *chai latte*? Despite similarities in spelling, some of those drinks taste and feel totally different. I had to order them separately, several days apart, to learn the difference the hard way. (I hate coffee, remember?)

So far, I have gotten my decaf right only once. Then again, not quite. After much rehearsal, I managed to put on a confident look and spit out the words in a neat sequence: "a tall, plain decaf, with no whipped cream, for here, please." To make my plan completely fail-proof — and protect my privacy in case of another fiasco— I adopted the most conspicuous alias, one anyone could relate to and spell correctly on my coffee cup: Daniel. The young lady behind the counter was speechless. Except for one last question which she insisted on asking —some unintelligible offer, which I declined.

Coffee was eventually served as it should be. Only the cup was inconveniently filled to the brim, forcing me to pour a third of it back into the trash container to accommodate some half & half. I ended up burning my hands and messing up big time. 'Not a problem. Not a problem', said a local helper as she rushed to my aid, soon adding, at a pace and accent I could now understand: "Next time she asks if you want room for cream, you'd better say yes."

Starbucks has done little to change my feeling about coffee. There is little hope it ever will, no matter how often I come back. Looking around for a hidden code did teach me a thing or two, though. Language choices are more arbitrary than one would think. Starbucks is probably unaware of the ordering anxiety their system inspires. Until they have put themselves in their customers' shoes, they will never know. Come to think of it, maybe they don't need to. Knowing you will keep trying their menu items at

The Language Game

your own expense is a justification as good as any other. Something else: most of us —my wife excepted— do not really care that much about coffee anyway.

The Starbucks code remains a mystery, but stubborn codebreakers believe it is just one cup away and keep reaching for that mug. Now, if you are still wondering what I really think about coffee after so many trips to Starbucks, review the preceding paragraph. The answer* is shouting at you, encoded in acrostic encryption. Do you see it? Here is a tip: focus on capital letters. By now, it should not surprise you.

*still sucks

No-Sense, No Deal

In early 2014, companies catering to an increasing international client base rushed to have their websites localized in as many languages as possible. They did so under the spell of a report from a US-based independent research firm specializing in global business.

Through surveys of over 3,000 consumers in non-Anglophone countries in Asia, Europe, and South America, *Common Sense Advisory* had established that over half (54.2%) of the people in these regions will only buy from websites where information is presented in their native language. And the demand for localized content increases to over 60% once you reach into specific countries such as France.

Results are even more telling when one compares the purchasing habits of consumers from different countries. Take Japanese and Spanish shoppers, for instance. The former are four times less likely than the latter to buy from English-only websites. The report title encapsulates it neatly: *Can't Read, Won't Buy.*

Curiously enough, the resistance to buy from English-centric sources had no direct correlation with one's command of English as a foreign language. Meaning that regardless of how well they understand or get by in

English, consumers still prefer to be addressed in their mother tongues.

Fast forward five years, and that rationale is now extending beyond the written word, as more and more meetings are pushed to the cloud and as businesses expand further into Southeast Asia or Africa. And here we have to ask ourselves: Are people easily dissuaded to buy or enter a deal if they are constantly spoken to in a language other than their own? Are companies leaving money on the table for insisting on meeting only in English, or German, or French?

Logic and emotion

Science —or plain commonsense anyway— seems to indicate so. In his book *Descartes' Error: Emotion, Reason, and the Human Brain,* neurologist Antonio Damasio sustains that people make logical decisions for emotional reasons. And nothing elicits emotion faster than language — particularly one's own—, as famously noted by Nelson Mandela: "if you talk to a man in a language he understands, that goes to his mind. If you talk to him in his own language, that goes to his heart." Conversely, there is no faster path to frustration than being unable to express ourselves thoroughly in a language we don't totally master. To use another quote —this time by an anonymous source— "when we speak a foreign language we say only what we can."

Professional language mediation —a.k.a., translation and interpretation— can arguably be traced back to those emotional and logical roots. Anger leads to poor business decisions. Inaccuracy usually results in losses. Yet, most companies still struggle in English-only conferences despite their international reach. Shouldn't they be localizing their meetings as they have their websites?

These observations, as somber as they sound, present an opportunity for the interpreting community, if we are able to put a price tag on the miscommunications in global business while demonstrating the cost-effectiveness of professional language mediation services.

The message is simple: misspeak, and you will overpay. But until we are able to assess and quantify the financial losses that come from single-language interactions, and how these losses are mitigated by the use of trained linguists, people will continue to hurt. And that includes us, linguists.

We tend to believe that English will get us through anything. But anyone who has ever been to Thailand or Vietnam knows how difficult it is to navigate the large metropolitan areas in those countries —or get a cab anywhere— without speaking at least some rudimentary Thai or Vietnamese (or without Google Translate, for that matter). Now imagine what it takes to close a deal involving hefty sums of money.

Well, imagining doesn't cut it anymore. It is about time we assessed the dollar cost of poor business decisions, including the decision not to engage interpreters, and the size of unrealized business from language-shy consumers.

The time for guesswork is long past. New, quantitative, data-driven analyses are needed. A new report must be commissioned. I am not the one to write it. But I can suggest a title: "No-sense, no-deal."

Juggling Two Languages at Once

In 1956, during a diplomatic reception in Moscow, Soviet leader Nikita Khrushchev told western bloc ambassadors – "Мы вас похороним!" His interpreter rendered that into English as "we will bury you!" This statement sent shockwaves through the western world, heightening the tension between the Soviet Union and the U.S., who were in the thick of the Cold War.

Some believe this incident alone set East-West relations back a decade. As it turns out, Khrushchev's remark was translated a bit too literally. Given the context, his words should have been rendered as "we will live to see you buried," meaning that communism would outlast capitalism – a less threatening comment. Though the intended meaning was eventually clarified, the initial impact of Khrushchev's apparent words put the world on a path that could have led to nuclear armageddon.

So now, given the complexities of language and cultural exchange, how does this sort of thing not happen all the time? Much of the answer lies with the skill and training of interpreters to overcome language barriers.

For most of history, interpretation was mainly done consecutively, with speakers and interpreters making pauses to allow each other to speak. But after the advent of radio technology, a new simultaneous interpretation system was developed in the wake of World War II. In the simultaneous mode, interpreters instantaneously translate a speaker's words into a microphone while he speaks without pauses. Those in the audience can choose the language in which they want to follow.

On the surface, it all looks seamless. But behind the scenes, human interpreters work incessantly to ensure every idea gets across as intended. And that is no easy task. It takes about two years of training for already fluent bilingual professionals to expand their vocabulary and master the skills necessary to become a conference interpreter.

To get used to the unnatural task of speaking while they listen, students shadow speakers and repeat their every word exactly as heard in the same language. In time, they begin to paraphrase what is said, making stylistic adjustments as they go. At some point, a second language is introduced. Practicing in this way creates new neural pathways in an interpreter's brain. And a constant effort of reformulation gradually becomes second nature.

Over time and through much hard work, the interpreter masters a vast array of tricks to keep up with speed, deal with challenging terminology, and handle a multitude of foreign accents. They may resort to acronyms to shorten long names, choose generic terms over specific, or refer to slides and other visual aids. They can even leave a term in the original language while they search for the most accurate equivalent.

Interpreters are also skilled at keeping aplomb in the face of chaos. Remember: they have no control over who is going to say what or how articulate the speaker will sound. A curve ball can be thrown at any time. Also, they often perform to thousands of people and in very intimidating settings like the UN General Assembly. To keep their emotions in check, they carefully prepare for an assignment – building glossaries in advance, reading voraciously about the subject matter, and reviewing previous talks on the topic.

Finally, interpreters work in pairs. While one colleague is busy translating incoming speeches in real time, the other gives support by locating documents, looking up words and tracking down pertinent information. Because simultaneous interpretation requires intense concentration, every thirty minutes, the pairs switch roles. Success is heavily dependent on skillful collaboration.

Language is complex. And when abstract or nuanced concepts get lost in translation, the consequences may be catastrophic. As Margaret Atwood famously noted, "war is what happens when language fails." Conference interpreters of all people are aware of that, and work diligently behind the scenes to make sure it never does.

Nice Trumps Nasty

For years, I would get off at Farragut West and take a longer route to work just to toss him a coin and listen to the sound of his trumpet on Lafayette Square. I could hear him from blocks away, as he greeted passersby with a voice as loud as his instrument and just as happy: "God bless. I love you. Have a lovely morning!"

I never asked his name, and he never knew mine, but many of my bleak winter mornings have indeed been made brighter by that old man in rags. I don't recall ever stopping for more than a few seconds, but I always felt lighter once I got on my way again, mindful of the warmth and scent of coffee radiating from my hands, looking up at the clouds in hopeful anticipation of a little blue sky.

Now, nice cost me a job once. A dream job, with the bells and whistles of a senior UN position. I am talking tax-free, high figures, diplomatic status, tuition reimbursement and six weeks of paid leave.

I had made the long and short lists, and was confident as I landed in the Hague for the final round of recruitment. An interview planned for 30 minutes went on for nearly an hour. I was well prepared and had done my homework. I dodged all of their bullets and even fired a few back. I was sure I was hitting every nail on the head.

Too sure, perhaps. Which might explain why I never saw it coming. Towards the end of the meeting, the most empathetic interviewer asked me this, through a genuine smile: "How would your friends describe you?" I will let you guess my answer. It is a four-letter word.

She and her colleagues retained their smiles and shook my hand politely as we parted ways. But the phone never rang. As it turns out, the court for which I was applying is busy trying to bring to justice and eventually send to prison mass murderers and dictators with private armies and vaults teeming with bribe money. I guess they just don't do nice. What was I thinking?

I eventually landed a job with a UN organization not too long after that, and my mood gradually improved under layers of rationalization. Who did they think they were?

I relocated to Geneva, and before long I found myself once again walking longer than needed, so I could go through the gate where Lourdes would greet me with a smile and where François would pull my leg about football, in his typical African accent. Their badges read 'Security,' but they did more than just keep you safe. They kept us all sane and got everyone off to a good start. Theirs is a thankless job, but one that helps make the organization less toxic, more productive, a tad nicer.

Past those gates, UN agencies, or the international courts, for that matter, are no different than most workplaces, with the good, the bad and every shade in-between. There is great collegiality and there is verbal abuse. There are random acts of kindness, and office politics that can fast devolve into backstabbing. Then

The Language Game

again, who needs nice?

I would argue we all do. We just don't realize it.

In times of police brutality, when politicians get elected on bravado, and where yelling gets deadlines met, most of us have learned to see politeness as wimpy and meek. We contemplate meanness as a shield worth wearing, despite the long-lasting harm it does to ourselves and others once the excitement of immediate gains fades away.

Nasty may get things done, but it also gets people reaching for their coat and hat. Like in the Hague, where the applicant who beat me to the job left before her full contract term. She was probably too nice, I'm thinking.

Anybody who has ever worked for a jerk understands the value of civility. It gets you out of bed in the morning ready to go an extra mile. It drives us beyond good enough. It clears up the air and prevents us from turning into another jerk. It gets results, too, and they tend to last longer, as do the people who bring them about. Nice draws us in and makes us stick around. Nice retrains. Nice retains.

Of course nice can also be an excuse out of a kitchen that just got too hot, an escape route back to the safety of one's old comfort zone. But it also keeps you true to your purpose, your true credo. It is the voice that tells you where to go once you realize you don't need nasty.

I eventually did. I quit that job, uprooted my family one more time and flew back across the ocean, on to new pursuits.

I now commute by car, so I am not often on the

subway. But I still take a detour and drive by Lafayette Square on occasion. The man and his trumpet are long gone, yet I hear his tunes. I hear his voice, too, against the tingling of coins being dropped on his shallow tin can. I flip an imaginary quarter in the air and silently send him love and gratitude. And every time, as if by miracle, my morning gets a tad brighter.

How Do You Do That?!

The conference opens with an address in a foreign language. The speaker launches headlong into a highly complex subject at breakneck speed. The talk is replete with terms whose spelling I can only guess, most of which encoded in the alphabet soup of acronyms. To make matters worse, he insists on cracking jokes as culturally-specific as they are untranslatable.

Settled into my booth at the back of the room, I diligently repeat every word, every idea in my language. I can't stop moving my mouth. My head is adorned with a pair of earphones and a microphone that make me look like a pop star. Separated from the audience by a glass partition, I am often the target of an occasional fleeting glance from spectators.

The speech ends, and a lively Q&A session ensues, forcing me to translate the audience's questions into a foreign language and the speaker's answers back into Portuguese. Fifteen minutes later, the linguistic shootout is suspended for a merciful coffee break.

I breathe a sigh of relief as I set down my headphones. I slip out of the booth, and an enormous sense of freedom washes over me. Still somewhat stunned and without a clear recollection of the last 40 minutes, I weave my way through the crowds that have inundated the lobby. At the buffet table, a woman approaches me. She has a headset in her hands, and the memory of my voice is probably still vivid in her ears. I anticipate a complaint and scan her face for any sign of dissatisfaction. But to my surprise, she congratulates me on the quality of my interpretation and then follows up with a question that has been nagging her since the beginning of the conference: "How do you do that?!"

The storytelling problem

In his thought-provoking book *Blink*, Malcolm Gladwell talks about what he calls the *storytelling problem*. He says human beings "are a bit too quick to come up with explanations for things we really don't have an explanation for." We are uncomfortable with not having rational explanations for what we do. We're left with a disturbing sense of uselessness, the impression that things happen by chance, that our performance is the result of sheer luck. Unable to deduce logical conclusions from evidence, we feel frustrated. And to escape that frustration, we tell a story. We devise a hypothesis and arbitrarily accept it as fact, soon clinging to that 'fact' as a way of giving meaning to what we do. We're not trying to conceal anything, nor are we pathological liars. It's just part of being human.

In the absence of an explanation that is even marginally believable, we turn to superstition, to a belief in some higher power or the so-called sixth sense. Gladwell cites the case of a fireman, whose intuition has saved him from potentially fatal accidents on numerous occasions. He always leaves a burning building seconds before tragedy strikes. Amazed, he attributes his miraculous escapes to some extra-sensory perception. That is the story he tells himself.

In interpretation, much remains to be explained. We don't know for sure which neurological phenomena make it possible for the brain to coordinate so many processes at once. It's as if the brain splits but at the same time is more connected than ever. And if it does split, it doesn't just split in two, but rather into multiple parallel brains that work on thousands of concurrent tasks of which we are hardly conscious.

Gladwell sheds new light on this phenomenon, exposing an adaptive unconscious that reasons at high speed using minimum information. That adaptive unconscious—not to be confused with the repressed unconscious described by Sigmund Freud—is what allows us to make such snap decisions. It operates according to mechanisms that are invisible to that part of our brain that wants an explanation for everything. But it works behind a locked door. It's fickle and reserved. It doesn't take kindly to invasions of privacy, nor does it offer up its secrets freely. It works best when left alone. It can't be drowned out by rational analysis, and it doesn't like being asked 'why?'

Interpreters are in a constant race against time. They live under pressure. They can't always afford the luxury of collecting massive amounts of information. They must edit, limit the number of options available and forgo lengthy word-choice processes. They have to be economical and objective. They have to be frugal. They have to do more with less. Our adaptive unconscious allows us to do just that.

Interpreting is making decisions, and good decision-making depends not on the volume of available information, but rather on our ability to extract the most meaning from the thinnest slices of reality. This is particularly important when faced with limitations of time, processing capacity, and content. It's something we do intuitively, from experience, without 'thinking.' It's what determines our good or bad feelings about a certain person or situation. That inexplicable attraction or deep-seated aversion may appear entirely random. But look closely, and you'll find that a core of invisible information conditions our first impressions. It may be a facial microexpression, or an unapparent similarity with some power figure, or a soothing voice leading us to recall select memories, or words evoking an emotional state to which we secretly aspire. Be that as it may, this information is transparent, something we perceive without seeing clearly, something unconscious.

Just like that fireman, you and I are gifted with alternative and unconscious rapid cognition mechanisms. Our ability to do often surpasses our capacity to explain why. *Homo faber* is capable of working independently. And *homo sapiens* is not omniscient, after all. The two walk side by side, but not always hand in hand. We need to give ourselves more credit and respect that fact. We need to stop telling stories.

Locking the brain out

Matters that involve what we would call insight follow a different set of rules. In these cases, thinking—that is, conscious thinking in a traditional sense—usually bogs us down.

Our intuitive mind extends beyond our brain, and at times even does without it. A classical guitarist is capable of executing from memory complex pieces learned through systematic practice. But, after a long period of inactivity, he will have a difficult time remembering a solo in its entirety. The first chords will come with ease, but at any moment, his fingers may get lost, and the rest of the piece won't be there. When that happens, reproducing the melody in one's head or analytically mapping the fretboard does little to bring back the lost notes. The solution musicians have discovered is to repeat the section they can remember over and over while deliberately trying to ignore the music. When they stop consciously trying to remember, as they relax and focus their attention elsewhere, without thinking or wondering why, the music returns. The hand comes alive, and it's the fingers that do the remembering. But for that to happen, the rational mind must be turned off. The door has to be shut. The brain must be locked out.

Even so, a word of caution is in order. Our unconscious mind may be autonomous and have a life of its own, but it doesn't always get it right. It lacks the cognitive environment previously created by our conscious attention. It relies on previously directed effort, systematic training, specific preparation, and accumulated experience. Left to its own devices, and without the counterpoint of reason and traditional knowledge, our unconscious tends toward more immediate stereotypes. It opens the door to our preconceptions, which quietly begin to dictate our choices and preferences based on false premises. It leads us to decisions that we don't understand. Our intuition can also fail us.

Effective decision-making requires analytical as well as emotional balance. In the interpretation booth, we often receive information from sources we are unable to identify. There are things we remember through conscious memorization and analogy. Other pieces of information come from a different kind of memory, where the mere sound of a word in a foreign language seems to unleash inferences that automatically lead to its equivalent in the other language.

Sometimes a shake of your booth mate's head or an almost imperceptible mouth or eye expression is all it takes to save you and bring just the right phrase to the fore. A casual reading of the program of a professional conference, minutes before it begins, or a stroll through the exhibit hall, can be the perfect complement to hours of preparation the night before.

Our capacity to capture information greatly surpasses our ability to explain why or how. In a sense, by need as well as intention, we learn partly by osmosis, extracting as much as we can from broken conversations and texts, in a hodgepodge of random elements that surprisingly come together a few hours later, during the conference.

Psychology is quite familiar with that effect of influencing or predisposing our mind to a specific type of knowledge or experience and can even induce it. It's known as priming. Like interpreting, it seems like magic. It can't work. It shouldn't work. And yet it does! We just don't know exactly how.

Once again, a word of advice seems appropriate here: before the session begins, regardless of how much preparation you have already done, flip through the program. Walk through the exhibition hall, if there is one. Stop at different booths. Talk to people. Ask questions, at the risk of sounding foolish. You don't really care about the answers. You just need the many technical terms recited back to you, terms that will probably come up in a presentation 15 minutes later. And on your way back to the booth after a coffee break, wander around to see what is on display. Do so to relax, just for the fun of it, not as a conscious preparation exercise. The results may surprise you.

The unconscious you

As it turns out, our intuitive mind extends beyond our brain and at times even does without it. Our unconscious perceives and processes many signals that our rational mind cannot. It reaches under the surface and breaks down a complex picture into minimum units of meaning, the thinnest slices of the whole, getting as close as possible to the basics, to the DNA, if you will, of a situation. And it brings us information coded in almost instinctive impulses to act.

In the interpretation booth, this process can take various forms: an unusual sense of comfort with a speech or a speaker, an almost telepathic rapport with your colleague in the booth, that wonderful feeling of being able to read the mind of another person, at times even guessing what she has to say. This is when we are able to shake off the literalness of a speech and reconstruct the ideas with our own vocabulary, expressing them as *we* normally would. This is when we are really interpreting, spontaneously and accurately, thanks to our surprisingly complete—and again inexplicable—understanding of a subject previously inaccessible to the unwashed.

We have this ability to read body language, to derive robust inferences from abstract concepts, to discern the intention behind a speech, to finish a thought based more on the feeling it inspires than on the words used to express it. We just have to think without thinking. All it takes is some balancing between the rational mind and that mysterious part of us that can make the impossible seem surprisingly trivial, that intuitive part of us that gets it right even when we may feel we are guessing. We know how to do it. We just don't know why.

According to Joshua Aronson, one of the researchers quoted in *Blink,* "people are ignorant of the things that affect their actions, yet they rarely feel ignorant." I couldn't agree more. Ultimately, how do interpreters manage to do what we do? Over the years, I have gathered many clues, but perhaps all I have done amounts to little more than storytelling.

In an effort to answer the question posed by that kind woman during the coffee break we shared so long ago, I have tried several keys to unlock the door. Despite my best efforts, it's still closed. All that is left is for me to accept Aronson's counsel and admit that the most honest answer I have to her question still is simply "I don't know."[2]

---

[2] Translated from Portuguese by Barry Slaughter Olsen.

INSIGHT

The Sound of Silence

The right word may be effective, but no word was ever as effective as a rightly timed pause.

— Mark Twain

From his mid twenties, Ludwig van Beethoven experienced a growing hearing impairment that would eventually leave him completely deaf. The progressive, humiliating condition didn't stop the German musical genius, who continued to compose poignant and beautiful music he could still hear in his mind. His late quartets, written during the terminal phase of his ailment, contained pauses that got arguably longer, as though to impart the composer's gradual drifting into a world of encroaching silence.

Considered by many to be Beethoven's best, these pieces introduce an unorthodox blend of short-ringing notes interspersed with longer-lasting pauses to enhance the melodic phrases resulting from their encounter.

Beethoven's pauses were clearly marked on the original sheet music as genuine 'notes,' true acoustic events. He would often position them at the end of a score, to be 'played' between the last sounded note and the double line that closes the bar, as if to gently usher the melody back into the silence from whence it came and without which there can be no music.

Like music, human speech, while arguably less likely to cause the same impact as Beethoven's enrapturing themes, is also a succession of audible phrases and inaudible fillers daisy-chained in a way intended to convey meaning and spur emotion. As in music, a crucial element is often overlooked in speech that is exactly what allows humans to make sense of—and relate to—any string of sounds or words: the pauses between them.

As blank spaces around words and paragraphs on a printed page, the gap between the sounds uttered by our interlocutors set the boundaries within which words, phrases, and sentences can take shape and morph into images in our minds.

Structurally speaking, the pauses in one's speech pattern are the mortar that keeps the building blocks of language together. Ultimately, how we lay those bricks, and the amount of plaster we employ, is what confers us intelligibility while tagging our unique phonic signature.

Pauses also serve a purpose beyond structure. They can be used for emphasis, dissuasion, reiteration, or as a means to assure one's understanding. They mark changes in pace or subject, and they grant those on the receiving end the necessary time to process content and appreciate form. Finally, a pause will give the speaker time to regain control and recollect his thoughts.

Few people enjoy listening to a speaker who will not stop to breathe, just like everybody dislikes a hesitant, back-tracking interpreter whose delivery is packed with audible fillers and static, in a low signal-to-noise ratio. While there is little you can do as an interpreter to fix an underperforming speaker, there are ways to ensure that his flawed rhetoric will not rub off on you and erode your credibility. Here are a few suggestions:

1. Start by questioning the typical interpreter's obsession with getting every word in. You're not a voice-over talent. If the original delivery is poor, shift your loyalty to content.

2. Next, lower the incoming audio feed to a comfortable level. Empirical evidence suggests that the louder the volume, the faster an interpreter will tend to speak.

3. Save for quotations, virtually any concept can be articulated in fewer words without sacrificing content. Cut through alliterations and mercilessly slash any unnecessary repetition. Look for acronyms and industry-accepted abbreviations. Saying E2 instead of *dihydrolipoyl transacetylase* takes a fraction of the time and may make just as much sense to a room of biochemists, especially a second time around.

4. Learn to identify crutches that could be dropped, such as phrases bearing little or no impact on substance (e.g., 'for whatever it is worth' or 'next slide, please').

5. Practice the use of adverbs such as thereby, hitherto, and therein. They may sound pedantic but will save you a ton of time if used correctly.

6. Provided they read well to everyone in the room, refer to slides, handouts, and other visuals or teaching aids containing long lists of items, names, or figures the speaker insists on spelling out.

7. Have shorter off-the-shelf versions for time-

consuming enunciations that may come up in every meeting. Saying 'the Minister is otherwise engaged' works better than listing a series of irrelevant excuses as to why Her Excellency is not in attendance.

As with any other tool in interpreting, mastering these suggestions takes time. It may also require a slight shift in how you look upon your role as an interpreter. To flatten the learning curve, practice rendering high-speed content in as few words as possible. Use the same audio feed repeatedly and take note of the strategies that work best for you.

Make silence your friend and pace yourself consistently. Whatever you do, refrain from asking the speaker to slow down, unless you appreciate hearing empty promises. He is not trying to upset you deliberately. His accelerated pace might be just a coping strategy for anxiety, and suggesting he change anything in his delivery is not just disruptive but pointless. Shouting at Beethoven for attention would be just as effective.

The Compassionate Interpreter

You most likely do not know him, although you probably should if you are a jazz fan.

He is a virtuoso instrumentalist who has been playing since age six. He has visited over 60 countries and performed at every major jazz festival on the planet. He has recorded with virtually every Brazilian pop singer plus some heavyweights on the international jazz scene. Blowing into his saxophone is the only thing Widor Santiago has ever done for a living. He completely masters his instrument and is at ease performing live before hundreds of thousands of spectators in large arenas or at Copacabana Beach during the now-traditional New Year's festivities in Rio.

Yet, despite his unquestionable experience and immaculate precision, Widor, now in his mid-fifties, still follows a rather strict ritual before stepping on stage. It includes introspection, concentration drills, and, quite surprisingly, prayers.

A comparable craft

Music is as complex a language as any other. It uses its an

ancient notation method of dots, bars, and symbols, a part of which got transliterated and simplified in modern times using the first seven letters of the Roman alphabet to refer to the seven basic musical notes. As with any spoken language, music is susceptible to infinite variations in tone, pitch, intensity, and tempo. In their urge to communicate, skillful musicians and interpreters will deftly combine those elements just so to disclose or conceal, enrapture or aggravate, grieve or celebrate, reveal or withdraw.

Musicians can be compared to conference interpreters on many counts: the former deal in musical notes and melodic phrases, the latter in words and units of meaning. For everything else, there are probably more similarities than there are differences.

A musician, like an interpreter, will rely heavily on a sense of hearing while keeping all other sensory channels open to any ancillary elements of meaning that could be blended into a harmonious whole: the conductor's gestures, the symbols on the score, the vibration given off by one's instruments, the audience's reaction. Interpreters and musicians must be endowed with a fine notion of timing, intensive focus, and agility. They must be agile and able to improvise at a moment's notice. They perform live in front of massive audiences, making endless instantaneous decisions as they give voice to other people's songs or tales.

The risks inherent in such high-visibility, live streaming performances can make stress a lifelong companion to musicians as well as interpreters.

Playing to transform

At first glance, Widor's pre-show routine does not quite

add up. After so many years on the road, you would expect an artist of his caliber to have overcome any performing anxiety or stage fright. Could he have butterflies in his stomach at every new gig? I was determined to find out, driven by something other than mere curiosity. I sought an analogy that could produce actionable advice one could put to good use on stage as well as in the booth. Taking advantage of my proximity to him —I married his sister some 30 years ago—I decided to ask him straight. An enlightening conversation ensued.

"I like to take a minute to remind myself of the reasons I am there," Widor explained, pausing briefly before continuing. "Different people play for different reasons. Some of my colleagues play from a place of anger. They resent being discriminated against, socially, racially, or otherwise. They feel they have been dealt a bad hand, and it makes them angry. They take that anger with them on stage and work extra hard to shine if only to take it out on the world."

He went on to explain that other performers play for the reassurance that comes with applause. They enjoy the boost to their self-esteem and capitalize on their insecurity to perform like never before and attract the recognition they crave. There are also those whose art is a form of avoidance. Their heart is no longer in it, but playing keeps them busy while providing a perfect excuse to procrastinate and stay away from something else they ought to be doing (but at which they secretly fear failing).

Widor's words totally and immediately resonated with the interpreter in me. In a profession as ego-driven as ours, it is easy to get misled. Breaking into the craft may at times involve a fair amount of elbowing, and the resulting anger can accompany a newcomer long after the initial friction. Also, simultaneous interpreting is still regarded as a superior skill, bordering on the magical, and the reassurance that comes from knowing one can do it and do it well may be uplifting and keep an interpreter elated for years on end. And there are many among us whose enthusiasm has faded, for whom playing has lost its luster. They feel jaded and yet unable to turn the table. Anxiety mounts.

"Anger can be as valid a driver as any other, provided the result is good music," Widor continued. "Still, in such circumstances, there will always be some underlying anxiety that is hard to push away," he warned.

Now, if the jitters are no longer a problem for Widor, then why all the introspection and praying before each of his performances? He settled the issue quite surprisingly. "I know that on any given day, in any crowd, there is at least one individual ready to be touched by a single note I play. I pray that she or he is there and leaves changed." He concluded the conversation with a powerful statement: "I play to transform."

For a more compassionate tune

Regardless of what we do, we are all moving along a continuum spanning the full spectrum of human feelings. And while any emotion can technically carry us forward and help us shine, some will leave a lingering, better aftertaste. The higher we move up the emotional scale, the closer we are to excellence and bliss. Learning to progress from mediocre to awesome and from miserable to great involves discovering loftier emotions from which to operate.

Anything worth doing is worth doing right. Interpreting should be no exception. It is a beautiful craft, ultimately anchored in the notion of service. It is also a stressful, taxing activity that can leave us mentally and physically drained, so we might as well do it for the right reasons. Why desecrate it with emotions unworthy of the effort? Why tie its expression to our need for reassurance or, worse yet, retribution? Why not make it meaningful by making it about someone else? Could we possibly transit from anger to vanity to detachment and, like Widor, eventually become more compassionate? It will likely be a gradual process, and the first step, of course, is determining where we find ourselves now. Looking for our underlying motives takes full precedence.

So, trying to translate into actionable advice some of what I learned from my friend that day, here are some suggestions and questions to help interpreters keep the reasons for their actions in check and evolving:

- Make it a habit of reflecting on why it is that you do the things you do.

- More specifically, try to drill down on what makes you tick. Be honest!

- Challenge your motives by asking what is next on the scale.

- What could make you want to perform better? What emotion could keep you going forever?

- For whom are you playing? Whom are you hoping to touch?

- What could take you to a more compassionate mode?

- How would that affect your anxiety?

These are hard questions, and the answers will likely elude you for a while. Yet asking them and acting on the ensuing hunches is the only way forward. In the meantime, you would do well to emulate part of Widor's compassionate routine. Taking a minute to remind yourself of the real reasons you are there will make you a more conscientious interpreter. You do not need to pray if you are not spiritually inclined, but a little introspection before opening the mic is easy enough to do and well worth your time.

Beyond the booth or across the stage are discoveries waiting to be made, insights dying to materialize, myths one push away from collapse. And in any crowd, on any given day, there is at least one life longing to be transformed. All it takes is one note played right, one word uttered purposefully, with precision and compassion.

Coping Tactics Revisited

> *The pessimist complains about the wind; the optimist expects it to change; the realist adjusts the sails.*
>
> — William Arthur Ward, writer

Upon setting sail from the Spanish port of Seville in 1519, Ferdinand Magellan was unsure of just what to expect. He had a hunch that he should sail west, believing this route would take him to the lucrative spices that grew in the Indies.

He took along the best technological and human resources available to him and left port with a flotilla of five ships loaded to the hilt with provisions, hoping for the best in a voyage whose duration he could not estimate. Under his command sailed a contingent of 260 men seduced by the promise of fortune and glory, their only chance to escape a miserable existence.

The captain-general would be up against more than just the ferocity of the southern seas. He had dared to question age-old tenets of pseudo-religious beliefs, and many among his peers were certain that despite his conviction, Magellan was attempting the impossible.

The intrepid navigator knew he would have to

prove the foolishness of countless medieval superstitions. Legends spoke of sailors swallowed up by boiling waters south of the Equator and of ships torn apart by magnetic isles that could pull the nails out from the hull. Ferdinand Magellan was a determined explorer, ready to put his life on the line. But he was also a man of the times and certainly not immune to the superstitions of the day.

The fear connection

Like sailors contemplating an imminent journey into uncharted waters, interpreters, too, have to grapple with a number of ghosts as they prepare for, and later reminisce about, their maiden voyage. Myths abound and are bred by ignorance and by panicky fantasies that tend to beset the unsure mind. Fear—be it endogenous or induced by circumstance—is how humans react to the unknown.

Yet, deliverance comes only from experience, and one has to muster the courage to set out to sea, hoping there is no cliff at the edge of the world after all. As they sail away from safe harbor, interpreters would do well to master at least some basic tricks while still ashore. So, lantern in hand, let us shed light on five important coping tactics[3] every interpreter should have in their toolbox as they prepare to weigh anchor.

1. **Simplifying discourse through acronyms and generalizations:**

   This common strategy, which soon becomes second nature, is a safe way to deal with speed, as it saves time

---

[3] For more coping tactics in interpretation, see Daniel Gile's *Basic Concepts and Models for Interpreter and Translator Training*, John Benjamins, 1997.

while preserving content. For example, the United Nations becomes UN; International Monetary Fund becomes IMF, and *pyruvate dehydrogenase* might be rendered simply as 'the enzyme in question.' The downside is that acronyms do at times get translated, and the effort required in realigning the letters may take longer than merely repeating a mouthful.

2. **Keeping a word or term in the original language:**

This is somewhat counterintuitive. Aren't interpreters supposed to translate every word? Well, not quite. Rather, their job is to convey ideas, which occasionally means recognizing which concepts are better left unchanged. But this tactic can also be used as a temporary crutch, in a fix, until a linguistic equivalent can be recalled for use a second time around. If relevant, the term will undoubtedly occur innumerable times and will eventually be rendered satisfactorily. If not, keeping it in the original language won't have been all that unforgivable.

3. **Changing the order of elements in an enumeration:**

Here's a rather elaborate yet advantageous strategy. Say the interpreter is lagging behind in a sentence as the speaker suddenly rushes through a long list of countries. Anticipating an imminent clogging of his short-term memory, the interpreter stores in his mind the first two or three names on the list and jumps straight to the ones being spoken next, which he renders immediately as heard. Once the list comes to an end, only the first few names he skipped need to be recovered from memory. The result is usually a 100% retrieval rate with zero overload.

4. **Reconstructing meaning from the context:**

   This is a dangerous yet useful tactic, where the loss of a word or idea is compensated for by the introduction of the most probable corollary to a preceding argument or semantic construct. At such times, besides their linguistic skills and their ability to improvise, interpreters rely heavily on extra-linguistic information (i.e., previous knowledge about the subject matter being discussed or the content they have gained in the course of the conference itself). This is time-consuming and requires a good sense of timing to be done correctly. Given the possible loss of content and the reputational risk, this tactic ought to be avoided to the extent possible. There will be situations, though, when nothing else works.

5. **Know when to acknowledge one's mistakes:**

   As much as we hate to admit it, interpreters do make mistakes, and handling them properly is an essential survival skill. It is also tricky. Saying 'sorry' or 'rather' may solve the problem of content, but it leaves the impression that the mistake was the speaker's and that she is the one apologizing.

   This tactic doesn't go unnoticed to more experienced interpreters, most of whom have occasionally passed blame in cases of immaterial omissions. Yet, when dealing with a severe misnomer or inaccuracy, ethics dictate that the interpreter rectify a potential misunderstanding, making sure to speak in the third person to avoid confusion. This momentary admission of guilt is important specifically to protect the speaker, and while it could potentially undermine the interpreter's credibility, it may also enhance it. Admitting a mistake denotes self-assurance. Working to fix it indicates conscientiousness.

Sailing on

The mechanisms listed above don't even scratch the surface, but they are a good starting point. To grow as an interpreter, one has to expand this repertoire of coping tactics while working hard to question any nonsensical myths. In a world long haunted by imaginary demons and shadows, lighting a candle still works better than cursing the darkness. The ghosts of our time must be challenged, one by one. And while these specters may impress us with their power, they are seldom unknown.

Other than scurvy, whose cause would remain a mystery for another three centuries, all of Magellan's adversaries were known and mighty—the violent seas, the raging storms, the mutinous sailors, the distance, the famine. The captain-general never did encounter boiling waters or magnetic rocks. When he finally succumbed while still *en route*, it wasn't in the jaws of a mythical sea creature. He actually got himself killed during an ill-considered and unnecessary show of force against a tribe in the Philippines.

Ultimately, Magellan's expedition paid a high price for challenging established myths and traditions. Four of five ships were lost, and over 200 men were killed. It was, by most objective standards, an utter failure. Yet it dismissed many of our fears and changed the world forever.

The Legacy of Jerome

Jerome, the illustrious theologian, and linguist we celebrate as the patron saint of translators may have been canonized after his death, but while he trudged the earth, his temper was rather unsaintly. His knack for languages was rivaled only by a talent for attracting trouble and making adversaries, often going several rounds with them regarding religious and linguistic issues.

His story is documented in the prolific correspondence he maintained with other elite thinkers of his time. Among the recipients of his missives were Saint Augustine, Popes Damasus, and Epiphanius, and Jerome's longtime friend, the Roman Senator Pammachius.

To the latter, he addressed one particular epistle that would be eternalized as the *Magna Carta* for translators. In the text, Jerome defends himself from the affronts of another reputable translator, Tyrannius Rufinus, who accused him of infidelity in rendering into Latin a letter from Pope Epiphanius to Bishop John. Given the Pope's reputation and the purity of his style, that letter was "wanted in all of Palestine, by the ignorant and the educated alike."

The translation in question had been commissioned by Eusebio de Cremona, "a man of no small estimation," yet unacquainted with the Greek language. At his special request, Jerome acquiesced to "simplifying the argument" to make it more readily intelligible and delivered the translation with the disclaimer that it be kept private. A year and a half later, Jerome's detractors, allegedly incited by Rufinus, managed to usurp the text and publicize it as a display of translator's neglect or mischief.

The letter to Senator Pammachius was a passionate legal defense. An irate Jerome distills his anger through a series of examples to emphasize that even the prophets and evangelists did at times detach from a literal interpretation of the scriptures. And while that allowed for stylistic adaptations, albeit foreign, it never compromised or belittled the sincerity of their purpose. The Letter to Pammachius stands out for the richness of its content and style. It is the ultimate affirmation of Jerome's erudition and competence as a translator and a vehement defense of good translating, which, he argues, must "render sense for sense, not word for word." It also sheds light on the ubiquitous criticism, spite, resentment, and other inimical feelings shared by Jerome's peers, which he seldom failed to reciprocate.

Sixteen centuries later, not everything has changed. Criticism and translation continue to walk hand in hand. Online and off, within the interpreting booth or beyond its confines, critics abound, and supporters are hard to come by. In interpreting, particularly, this chronic lack of constructive feedback, coupled with an absence of objective assessment parameters, fuels a peculiar and vicious cycle where interpreters often gauge their performance relative to that of their booth mates. In such circumstances, criticism becomes the tool of choice for an instant ego boost. Pushing others down is the quickest way to feel good about ourselves, providing a platform on which to stand tall.

It doesn't help when one considers that the noble craft of simultaneous interpreting came to the fore in the wake of World War II, on a continent devastated by the banalization of violence. So widespread and unprecedented had been the nature and reach of the atrocities perpetrated that a new word had to be minted to qualify them: genocide.

Despite the mounting empirical evidence and the unflattering historical roots for such belligerent disposition, the animosity experienced and spread by Jerome, and the ripples it might have sent across time, need not be replicated ad infinitum in our stuffy glassy booths or among our peers. Peace can and should be restored. It is long overdue.

Now, talking about peace is tricky, and it doesn't take much to come off as righteous, pompous, or silly. It all sounds grand and out of reach. Yet, the type of peace we're aiming for here—collegiality—is easy enough to reinstate. All it takes is an iota of self-awareness and an extra vigilant disposition. To try and make it less abstract, here are five detox strategies you can try to start transcending Jerome's legacy:

1. **Focus on the positive**

    Look for and praise the types of behavior you'd like to see more of. What we concentrate on grows.

2. **Pay it forward.**

    Pave the way for more positivity by being the first to offer encouragement and compliments. Do so unconditionally as well as sincerely.

3. **Make no excuses.**

    We all have bad days. Own your occasional shortcomings. Offer no justification and don't look for consolation in somebody else's actual or projected poor performance. Review the experience honestly in search of pointers as to what might have tripped you up. Then fix it.

4. **Shrug it off.**

    If a frustrated colleague finds fault with you or criticizes your performance, take the high road. If there is any truth to what they're saying, consider Step 3 above, and thank him or her.

5. **Cut yourself some slack.**

    Translation is, by design, an imprecise exercise. In our business, perfection is not only elusive but outright unattainable. Do your best and forget the rest. By acknowledging and accepting your limitations, you become more tolerant with others.

Adhering to the steps above will not make you a saint in the afterlife, but it will certainly warrant you a better experience in the here-and-now.

As for Jerome, learn to love him for his invaluable contribution to our craft and for thinking through some of the hard problems way before us. As to anything else, don't get involved. Leave it for Jerome and Rufinus to settle in eternity.

The ABC of United Nations

Since the release of my video[4] on the language requirements for interpreters in the United Nations (UN), I've been contacted by many aspiring interpreters with questions that are more or less the same.

Basically, they want to know whether they qualify, and they also wonder what else they could/should be doing to merit consideration as a future UN interpreter. At some point in their messages, they'll offer their own elaborate plan to learn this and that language and travel to this and that place.

The latest of such emails—and by far the most gracious—came from Hai, a young man from China/Singapore. After passionately sharing his benign obsession for languages in general and for interpreting in particular, he outlined his game plan:

> *I have a strong mastery of both **English** and **Chinese** (I grew up bilingual), took a fair amount of **French** and a little bit of **German** in college, self-studied **Japanese** and **Korean**, and have been trying to beat the unfamiliar*

---

[4] *So You Want to Become a UN Interpreter.* Available online at http://bit.ly/UN_TED

Cyrillic *script into my head (…) One of my personal goals in life is to master* **six languages**, *although I know that is more my ambition speaking than cool-headed thinking.*

Note that in one paragraph Hai tries to squeeze all six languages he believes he'll need to break into the UN, *plus* Russian as a backup. And while I fully understand and sympathize with his desire to have it all (haven't we all been there?), the irony is that as far as the UN is concerned, Chinese and English is all he would ever need (to qualify as a Chinese interpreter).

Hai's approach springs from a skewed yet popular notion that more languages—even non-UN languages—may somehow compensate for a less-than-ideal mastery of the few that do count.

The ABC system

What Hai and many others fail to realize is that working as an interpreter for the UN—whether as a freelancer or staff interpreter—isn't for everyone. Regardless of how good you are as an interpreter, you'll only be considered if you understand and adapt to the specific language requirements of the job.

In the high-end conference environment of multilateral organizations such as the UN, the European Institutions, and the Bretton Woods organizations, you're only supposed to interpret into your native languages. How you can use the other languages under your belt varies, in a greater or lesser degree, according to several factors. To better grasp this concept, one first needs to understand the ABCs of language classification used in professional interpreting circles:

The Language Game

- **A language** is usually the language you were born into (a.k.a., your native language). It could also be your primary language of schooling if your education—from high school and beyond—was completed in a different language. It's a language you totally master and can use confidently and correctly in formal or informal settings. A few interpreters will have two A languages.

- **B language** is a language you understand and speak fluently, but which is still a foreign language to you nonetheless. It's usually a language you learned in school or through on-off interactions and experiences in a foreign linguistic and cultural environment. For use in the booth, a B language must be one you speak impeccably. It's a language you can interpret from as well as into (under certain circumstances).

- **C language** is a language you understand, but one you're not entirely comfortable speaking. C languages are usually numerous, and in time, it's easy for interpreters to increase their repertoire of passive languages. These are languages one will interpret from, but never into.

In interpreting, less is usually more. And the reason is simple: focus! To excel as an interpreter, you need to tell the core from the fringe, sort the wheat from the chaff. Only after you've discarded what you don't need can you commit all you have into whatever is left. And believe me, to excel at that level, it will literally take all you've got.

That need to focus continues to hold true when it comes to choosing your working languages. You'll need to increase your knowledge and vocabulary exponentially in the languages upon which you rely in the booth. In that context, it would be wise to limit their number. At least while you're trying to break into the UN.

Now that number will vary depending on the booth you are targeting. For example, to qualify as a staff English booth interpreter in the UN setup, you must have either Spanish or Russian as a passive language (i.e., C-level), in addition to French. The same holds true for French booth interpreters (in this case, with the addition of English). This is done to minimize relay, the system whereby interpreters will interpret from other interpreters if they don't understand the language spoken on the floor.

Now as a future Chinese interpreter, our good friend Hai will only need two active languages to qualify as UN material: an A-level Chinese and a B-level English (or French). The same can be said of Arabic interpreters. They need a native command of Arabic and a competent, strong command of either English or French. Adding a few more passive UN languages would certainly help and make him more versatile, but isn't a requirement.

Some advice

With that in mind, the advice to Hai, and which you may apply to yourself, is to take the easy route:

> *Flex your Chinese and English muscle exclusively for some time, until you qualify as a Chinese interpreter.*
>
> *If you're more comfortable in English, then you'll need to polish your French and hammer that Cyrillic script twice as fast into your skull. Few pleasures compare to the joy of being able to converse, read, and interact in beautiful and complex languages such as Korean, German, and Japanese. Yet as non-UN languages, they will do little to nothing in*

helping you materialize your dream.

Also, do invest in that master's degree. Long gone are the days where self-taught interpreters could easily break into the big league. Look for a reputable school and give it your best. Not only will you learn new things, but you will also enlarge your circle of influence, guaranteed.

Finally, dear Hai, do forgive me for using your message and concern publicly to make a point. Rest assured nothing in my feedback is meant to discourage you. On the contrary. With your drive, it won't be long before you become a UN interpreter in your own right. See you in New York. or Geneva, for that matter.

Through the Looking Glass

They are easy to spot. Capricious, over-demanding interpreters for whom nothing is ever right: the pay is meager, the hours are long, the tasks are boring, and the coffee is not fresh enough. Judgmental and vocal, they are constantly scanning their surroundings for colleagues or circumstances to blame for their misery.

While some are excellent at what they do, most grossly overestimate their own abilities. These chronic attention-seekers make poor booth mates because of their propensity to compete rather than collaborate. Despite telling evidence, they will hardly ever acknowledge a mistake. It will always be *your* fault or mine. And they will surely rub it in.

These colleagues respond to life's many blessings with a feeling of entitlement rather than gratitude, and no matter how generous their lot, it's never enough. Life owes them a buck, and so do you.

Such attitude—exaggerated here for the sake of argument—is usually rooted in unconscious insecurity. It's the machinations of an ego that feels threatened and unspecial, and that will do anything to create some separation from the ordinary. It stems from a broken sense of self that has the notions of being and doing all twisted.

Deep down, we all like to think we're good and sensible. We root for the good guys in movies and are unanimous in condemning blatant acts of injustice. No one thinks of themselves as cruel, mean-spirited, cold, or unappreciative. Oh, we're not *that*. Yet a quick look around proves that we all can exhibit such behavior on occasion if the wrong buttons are pushed. We just don't bring ourselves to admit it often.

It is always easier to see and condemn misconduct in others. Hence the constant criticism and finger-pointing. It's a projection whereby the unconscious mind provides us with a tilted mirror image against which to vent and direct our anger, all the while fooling ourselves that the silhouette reflected back at us is not our own. This mechanism is meant to protect us.

At the end of the day, other people's behavior will always change in response to what they get from us. Again, we tend to take the reflection as reality, never looking at the true source of light.

We all know a few self-important interpreters who cannot be pleased. Yet in their hearts, they all think of themselves as nice people, no matter how unbearably obnoxious they may seem to the rest of us.

So, if too many arrogant divas are popping up in your booth, perhaps it's about time you take a long, good look at the image reflected back at you on that glass. Here are a few subtle points to ponder as you talk to yourself:

- Who do you blame when circumstances don't conform to your expectations?
- Do the words 'always' and 'never' pop up in your head or slip out of your mind often?
- Does your performance determine how you

feel about yourself?
- Are you in a silent competition with your booth mate?

The answers to the first two questions will tell you how personal, permanent, and pervasive you perceive the annoying circumstances in your life to be. The final two will show you how much of your identity you have wrapped around what you do, rather than who you are.

The exercise will expose beliefs and circumstances that may be triggering you off your best behavior. It will show areas where there may be room for improvement. Most importantly, it will make you a better and more conscientious interpreter that clients and colleagues would want to have around.

Give it a try, and you may find yourself wondering whatever happened to those prima donnas.

Mind Your Language, You @#x!$%*!

In late 2017, I was interviewed by the BBC in connection with an incident involving the interpreter who watered down parts of President Trump's speech at the UN General Assembly that were critical of the Iranian regime. Transcriptions of both the original and the interpretation can be easily found online.

The interpreter was severely criticized on social media but stood his ground by indicating, *inter alia*, that he didn't feel he had the right to trash his own country on air.

BBC wanted to hear the perspective of a UN interpreter. They wondered whether linguists are at liberty to introduce such willful meaning shifts. I went as far as I could within the limits of a live interview but stopped short of passing judgment.

The following day, a few colleagues reached out to respectfully disagree with my approach, expressing the view that it's not an interpreter's job to decide what should or should not be said and that I would do well to condemn that attitude publicly. Basically, their point is that if somebody calls you a @#x!$%* in a different language, you have the right to know what they mean.

I hear them, and as a practicing interpreter and

longtime trainer of interpreters, I fully subscribe to that philosophy. In an ideal world, fidelity should trump political correctness any day. Interpreters should remain as neutral a conduit as possible and get the message across as heard. Then again, the world is far from ideal, and I also know that circumstances play a role.

Granted, such omissions and meaning shifts, if deliberate, would have been unforgivable coming from a staff interpreter working out of a UN booth. That was not the case, though. And that changes the game on many levels.

The fell clutch of circumstance

Culture is a huge factor in how one uses language. It plays a particular role in determining what one may say in public and how. What is considered appropriate or acceptable in a given country may be off-limits in another.

Many countries even have laws criminalizing the use of inappropriate language on television or radio. And please don't be too quick to dismiss this is as an attribute of some backward, fundamentalist nation. The example that springs to mind probably hits a lot closer to home:

> *Title 18 of the United States Code, Section 1464: Whoever utters any obscene, indecent, or profane language by means of radio communication shall be fined under this title or imprisoned not more than two years, or both.*

I guess the trick lies in determining who defines what is 'obscene, indecent, or profane' and how. Once again, the point at which strong language becomes 'profane' will vary drastically from one culture to the next.

Contrary to conventional wisdom, not every

culture requires a bad word to be present for the purposes of an insult. Again, the U.S. is a good example. Take 'son of a bitch,' for instance, where the insult is conveyed primarily by intonation and by the general understanding surrounding a euphemism where 'bitch' (female dog) is used to mean something other—arguably far worse—than an animal epithet.

In some cultures, the mere mention of someone's family or the use of taboo words like 'cancer' can come across as incredibly insulting, depending on the context. The same goes for waving, pointing fingers, or inadvertently exposing the sole of your shoe in public. If you are away from home, chances are those gestures, and a few of your words, might be taken harshly, offensively, or both.

It should be noted that the considerations above apply to individuals as well as cultures. That being so, an interpreter *may* feel personally offended by the use of particular language, for moral or religious reasons, and consequently inclined to substitute what he considers offensive with a less impacting speech when given a chance. Is he in the wrong for doing that? If so, according to whom and, more importantly, where?

Finally, this discussion would be incomplete if it fails to address a massive elephant in the room: the client. Who is the interpreter working for? Where does his loyalty belong? Once again, circumstances play a role.

His master's voice

As discussed briefly during the interview, most heads of state have their interpreters in tow when attending an international function. They do so for a couple of reasons.

First, they need to be certain they are getting a full and accurate rendition of what they are being told by their counterparts in an exchange—especially if someone is calling someone else a @#x!$%*.

Second, they rely on their interpreter to get their own message across as intended (which, mind you, may and often does differ from how it's said). Rather than a mere conduit or linguistic facilitator, the interpreter becomes a trusted adviser, a vital public relations official, who will try hard to help the president or prime minister stay objective and politically correct while delivering the message as briefed.

Under such circumstances, or under duress, one's perception of accuracy and fidelity might become more fluid, and the interpreter may find himself making slightly vaguer statements, either consciously or unconsciously, while giving the speaker a chance to rephrase the original utterance. One must be very clear about the job at hand. Then again, for a personal interpreter to a celebrity or public figure, that *is* the job at hand.

Yes, we can!

As a rule, freelance or staff interpreters are ethically obliged to say it as it is. We're not in the business of sugarcoating and not at liberty to deviate from the language chosen by the speaker as a matter of personal choice or whim. Then again, a personal interpreter is not exactly a freelance interpreter. The former is no longer a totally independent player and will be faced with decisions with which the rest of us will seldom have to contend.

In any event, the circumstances discussed above are scarce and specific, and adjustments, if any, will be minor, like finding substitutes for politically incorrect expressions or offering neutral pleasantries in lieu of compliments that could be taken the wrong way (when truly meant as compliments). These circumstances pose a conflict to any interpreter, whose ethics and credibility also hang in the balance. Not an easy job under any circumstances. And it doesn't get any easier when your audience reaches the millions.

As a freelance interpreter, I can choose who I work for, and I can object to impositions from a dictatorial leader whose ideas I don't share. Staff interpreters are not at liberty to make the calls alluded to here, and they can bask in the knowledge that full neutrality is what is expected of them.

That was not so for the Iranian interpreter in question, working as he was for a state-controlled national television chain in his country, and under clear and specific instructions. Given the circumstances, laws, and impositions mentioned above—whether written or not—neutrality was probably not an option. And while we can take issue with some of those impositions, we have to assume not everyone can.

Biofeedback For Booth Jesters

If you have been a conference interpreter long enough, chances are you may have found yourself in a situation where comments or jokes shared privately with a partner in the booth eventually got across to the audience.

I once had it happen twice in a single week. Luckily, I was only making suggestions to my booth mate. It was not like I was clowning around, foolishly pretending to speak German in front of a composed delegate standing across the window from us who, rather than suffer through my jokes, simply wanted to remind me that the event had started and that it was no longer time for a mic check. That was the day before.

Interpreters' consoles —the little switchboards we use to activate our microphones, select our incoming languages, and outgoing channels— can be tricky. They come in all shapes and sizes. 'Cough' buttons —used to pause the interpretation for whatever reason– can go by different names like 'mute' or 'off.'

Color codes for microphones vary, too. Most mics will turn red when active and green when off (go figure). Others will alternate between amber (on) and green (off). On a dual-mic console, placing the mic switch in the middle position may cut off or activate both mics, depending on the make and model. Some old shared consoles have individual cough buttons that, surprisingly, work only on one's own microphone. Your colleague's mic will continue to capture whatever you say, even with your cough button down. That was precisely what tripped me up that day.

Whatever their cause, these mishaps drive a vital point home: jokes and derogatory remarks have no place in the booth. Nor do idle chitchat or utterances of frustration at a speaker's high speed or incoherence.

In this context, the advice below may save us all some embarrassment in the future:

- Resist the temptation to be funny in the booth. Limit your comments to the absolute minimum once the meeting has been called to order or whenever your booth equipment has been switched on. When hundreds of heads turn back to locate you in the booth, let it be for the right reasons.

- Test your equipment first, and do not try to learn as you go. Make sure you get thoroughly acquainted with its many features.

- Make a point of testing every button if you have not seen that type of equipment before.

- Make a point of testing every button *even if* you have seen and worked with that type of equipment before!

- All good things come to early risers (a lesson I learned the hard way, given my typical Brazilian punctuality).

The Language Game

Let me reiterate this last point: be sure to come in early and test your every move before you go live so that you can start strong. The first five or ten minutes of a conference are crucial for an interpreter. It is your only chance to make an excellent first impression. It is your chance to build rapport and offer listeners a reliable delivery that is easy on the ears. It is not a good time to mess around. Once lost, this rapport and confidence may be hard to regain, especially if everyone has heard you acting like a bozo.

But if, like me, you cannot help playing the jester once in a while, here is something else you may want to try. It is a trick I learned from a good friend and mentor.

Have a receiver with you in the booth and an earbud that you can place under your interpreter's headset to hear your own interpretation. Volume should be kept as low as possible. This adds a layer of complication to an already complicated equation. It takes some getting used to, but it can be a life-saving device for forgetful types.

I can think of at least three benefits:

- It allows you to monitor what listeners are getting out there.
- It also helps you modulate and spare your voice, speaking softly yet ensuring proper delivery.
- It makes you aware of any interference or unwanted noises you might be producing while scratching your face, smacking your lips, or swallowing water.

Think of it as a form of biofeedback loop for funny interpreters. Make sure you allow several days for practice if you intend to experiment with this. The system, though effective, can be distracting to some.

Of course, you do not have to try my system. You can

create and enforce your own protocol for when shoot happens. Better yet: you can develop a system to ensure it does not occur in the first place.

For the technology-averse among you, here is a time-tested, low-tech variety that will likely yield the same results: keeping quiet until it is time to start interpreting.

The Fine Art of Blowing It

Here's what I did right: I watched the videos in advance and thoroughly reviewed the text. I researched the terminology and even put together a neat glossary. I made a point of meeting with Dr. Brahma in person minutes before his presentation, and got to review his every slide. I got him to clarify all the acronyms, obscure terms, and African names. My prep work had been spot on. I was ready to shine.

Here's what I did wrong: I never bothered to ask for the MC's script. I forgot to check the evening's program. I forgot to approach the host, even after we shook hands. I got too confident, thinking that if I was ready for Dr. Brahma, I was prepared for anything.

Here's where I blew it: I volunteered to go first, confident that I could set the pace for my booth mates, even knowing that Spanish was still a C language for me. Why not?!

Here is a few reasons why not:

- Because Dr. Brahma might not have a chance to speak for the first fifteen minutes.

- Because the host who was supposed to introduce

the speaker might spend a full quarter of an hour talking about something other than the subject I had so thoroughly researched.
- Because he might get carried away and go on forever, hypnotized by the sound of his own voice, in the process consuming my entire shift in light-speed announcements and calls to prospective members.

- Because assuming introductions are always going to be swift is just that: an assumption.

- Because I failed to grasp the real purpose behind the meeting.

That's why!

By the time Dr. Brahma walked to the podium, I had long walked away from my seat, in frustration. If only this had been Portuguese. Anyway... a few lessons learned:

Don't let it go to your head. Play conservative. Keep a low profile as long as you can. Hope for the best, and prepare for the worst. Make sure the ball is on your side of the court. *Then* smash it.

Or else, just blow it... like I did!

7 Things a Chief Interpreter Wishes You Knew

There are arguably some disadvantages to being a chief interpreter. One does not get to interpret as often. One has a clock to punch, reports to write, long staff meetings to sit through, and scores of managerial chores that are not necessarily fun. And while one free-rides occasionally on collective success, failure is no longer circumscribed to one's own mistakes. If an interpreter on my team falls flat on his face, I have a lot of explaining to do.

Obviously, the job comes with many perks. You are suddenly cleared into circles you did not know existed, where guidelines are discussed and decisions made that have a direct impact on working conditions, technology transfer, and the overall pace of progress in the industry. The opportunity to help shape the field of interpreting and leave the profession better than you found it is real. And did I mention the welcome promise of a steady income to weather the seasonality of freelancing?

But beyond the evanescent elite membership privileges and pecuniary incentives, what I like most about being a chief interpreter is the amazing learning experience it provides. It is the different outlook that comes from being on the other side of the counter while knowing full well what it is like to be a freelancer. It gives you an entirely different perspective. It tells you a lot about diversity and human nature while revealing many attributes of your own personality, some reassuring, and some you would rather sweep under the rug.

Now, just over two years into the job, I realize many things I wish I had known in my days as a freelancer. Knowing then what I do now would have significantly improved my performance and earned me an extra buck in the process. So, for the benefit of those freelancers who do not aspire to become chief interpreters, I thought I would share some valuable lessons learned from the perspective of a chief interpreter.

1. Quality Is a Package

One's interpreting abilities, accuracy, and smooth delivery rank high up on any chief interpreter's checklist. But so do punctuality, teamwork skills, flexibility, and, most importantly, manners— both in and out of the booth. The best interpreters are the ones who get the job done unassumingly while making it easier for everyone to do the same, including the chief interpreter. They work diligently on their languages as well as their people skills. By contrast, arrogant, over-demanding colleagues make it all about themselves and risk having relative gains in performance (if any) overcast by the toxic atmosphere they end up creating. All things considered, I guess any chief interpreter would prefer a good interpreter with a great attitude over an excellent interpreter with a poor attitude.

The Language Game

Take-home point: be good, but be nice.

2. It is About Peace of Mind, Not Razzmatazz

You have every reason to be proud of your skills and achievements. You worked hard on yourself and attained a reputation as a reliable, competent linguist. You interpreted for J.K. Rowling, Harry, Dumbledore, and got a standing ovation at Hogwarts. Kudos to you! Your VIP list will earn you extra credits with a prospective client and is certain to be a sensation among your Facebook friends. Yet being on a first-name basis with Lord Voldemort does little to impress chief interpreters. They have been around the block once or twice on that broom, too, and can quickly see through the self-promotion blabber.

To really leave a mark, review the attributes discussed in item 1. Prepare and deliver as a dependable professional. Get in, get it done, and get out. Do so consistently and let your work speak for itself.

Take-home points: drop the hocus pocus and sell the steak, not the sizzle.

3. A Fusillade of Questions Will Backfire

There are some valid questions an interpreter might consider asking before an assignment if the requirements have not been communicated effectively by the chief interpreter. Dropping a line to flag a vital omission or to seek clarification on the venue, the time, or the subject matter shows professionalism and conscientiousness. Overdoing it will convey the opposite impression, though, and you will come across as an inexperienced or, worse, insecure interpreter. To make sure this does not happen to you, here is a quick guide to getting the information you need in a manner which conveys professional competence.

- Think of all the questions you want to ask and then refine the list, mentally or on a sheet of paper.

- Strike out from your inventory any questions you might find the answers to somewhere else. (Unless a Sandy-like storm is anticipated, I have no idea what the weather will be like in Geneva next week, and I am not the one to tell you what to pack in your suitcase.)

- Drop the awkward requests. (No, I cannot get you a window seat on your upcoming trip to Moscow.) Also, refrain from asking questions to which answers have been promised. ("You said the program would be forthcoming. Any chance I could have it now?")

- Do not ask questions a chief interpreter might prefer not to answer, like who your boothmate is going to be or why you have not been assigned to interpret at the closing ceremony. You may end up with a vague answer or one you do not want to hear.

- Most importantly, in the event you receive a notification canceling the assignment (which can happen abruptly), be careful not to ask for reasons based on unproven assumptions. ("Did I do anything wrong?") Just reply with a short, assertive note to acknowledge the cancellation and reiterate your willingness to be of assistance a second time around.

- If you must rely on e-mail, please do your share to keep message traffic to a minimum. E-mail is an incredibly time-consuming tool. Keep your notes short and concise.

  If reacting to a group e-mail, do not copy everybody by clicking the 'Reply to All' button, and by all means, do not put anyone in blind copy. Whenever possible, present all relevant concerns in one single, concise e-mail and make it such that no reply is necessary. ("If I do not hear from you by Monday, I will assume ...").

Take-home point: Don't seek and ye shall find!

4. Ask and You May Well Receive

On the bright side, interpreting is a recession-proof occupation. The deeper the crisis, the more people talk about it. In every language. On the not-so-bright side, conference interpreting is seasonal by definition. Conferences follow a predictable ebb and flow pattern. For example, few people will be willing to meet over the holiday season and come August, it will be too damn hot (or cold) to talk about anything. You might as well close the talk shop for a good 30 days and be out playing golf or skiing.

But if you are a well-established professional in your area (geographically or otherwise), you can rely on a somewhat steady flow of contracts and income from February to mid-July and from September to early December. During those peak periods, you will run into a different type of problem: you will probably end up receiving too many work offers. Despite appearances, this is not a good problem to have. Save for occasional double-dipping, you can only service one conference a day. Unless you run a business where you capitalize on somebody else's labor, a sudden downpour of gigs after a long dry streak might get you wet, but it is unlikely to leave you dripping with gold. Somewhere along the line, you will have to sacrifice a full week of meetings for a conflicting two-day conference.

Regardless of how good you are, there will eventually be unwanted holes in your calendar. That is just a fact of life; a freelancer's life, anyway. While this situation just has to be accepted, that does not mean you have to take it lying down. During the low tides, most interpreters respond passively, sitting by the phone with their fingers crossed and wondering why it will not ring. They are too shy or too proud to make their availability known, and only a few will break the inertia and ask their employers for work. Guess what? These selected few who take the initiative are the reason your telephone is not ringing.

A chief interpreter will typically draw from a pool of hundreds of interpreters, who are continuously screened for quality, teamwork abilities, and availability. In times of plenty, everyone gets their share. But when conference days start to dwindle, you will need one additional attribute to keep the offers coming: visibility. I can only hire you if I *see* you. To be in my booth, you need to be on my radar screen. To keep coming back, you need to be top of mind.

There is nothing wrong with flagging your readiness to an employer. The trick is doing it nicely, without imposition. Do not ask funny questions and do not kiss up. Simply reiterate your willingness and availability in a concise, straightforward e-mail, with no attachments. You are not begging for work. You are presenting yourself as a viable option. In so doing, you increase your chances of landing another contract while helping your client in the process.

Take-home point: out of sight, out of mind.

5. Nobody Likes Whiners

In an ideal world, presenters speak slowly, bring extra hard copies of their presentations, and throw candies to interpreters from behind the podium. Schedules are announced in advance and kept unchanged. Travel conditions are excellent, the sound system works to perfection, and everyone around you is cool, calm, and collected. But save for Shangri-la, that is certainly not the norm anywhere, and the ensuing uncertainties often drive interpreters to the edge.

Some colleagues react to the added stress by going into chronic whining mode. Their frustration mounts and is often misdirected at teammates or the client. This leads to poor team spirit and puts people off fast.

As a conscientious colleague, you will want to keep a constructive attitude despite any perceived risks and would do well to put the client first. Be transparent. Address problems directly and be sure to target behavior, rather than people. Be part of the solution or be neutral. Not getting in the way is sometimes the greatest help of all and the kindest thing to do. Cursing the darkness may feel good and temporarily appease your anxiety, but lighting a candle works a lot better for all concerned.

Take-home points: reach for those matches and don't put oil in the fire.

6. Appreciation Goes a Long Way, Both Ways

The words 'thank you' are among the first and last ones to ever come out of an interpreter's mouth in the booth. They are also the first and last words they will hear as speakers open and close their presentations. Repetition alone should have by now engraved in our brains the self-evident truth that appreciation ought to precede and succeed all our actions. Sadly, however, that awareness is lost to many among us once we step out of our glassy working cubicles, and most interpreters leave those powerful words unsaid.

These colleagues waste a golden opportunity to experience a superior emotion and the promise of more good things to come. They overlook and eventually banalize the many blessings involved in bringing another day of work to fruition. They deny themselves the gift of joy and snap back into anxious anticipation for what tomorrow will bring. And tomorrow keeps bringing more of the same.

According to most ancient traditions, our universe runs on thought-forms and feelings, and what we call reality is a mere reflection of that which we project. In less esoteric lingo, science points in the same direction, with expectations dictating results in recent high-level experiments in Physics. Whether or not you believe in the magnetic pull of gratitude, adopting a more appreciative stance is guaranteed to make you happier. It will also bring you more jobs and ultimately, money. Another simple principle is at play here: reciprocity. Appreciation acknowledges the circumstances that bring freelancers and employers together, mindful that both parties could have chosen otherwise. Appreciation operates from the premise that both sides want to get it right. Appreciation acknowledges one's honest efforts, albeit imperfect, as steps in the right direction. It makes visible and reinforces that which need not be fixed. It feedbacks on itself and keeps mutually appreciative players engaged in a long, self-sustaining virtuous cycle.

Unless you cannot possibly accommodate any more prosperity or happiness than you currently have, you may consider increasing your thankfulness. Train yourself to feel grateful for —not entitled to— the offers of work you get. Acknowledge them with gratitude or decline with grace. Reinforce the behavior you want to see more of. Make it a habit to send a thank-you note to those who help you materialize the beautiful life you create for yourself in your chosen field. The trick is doing it in all sincerity, with conviction yet no expectation of receiving anything in return. No need to get carried away or say much. Those two simple words will do.

Take-home point: just say the word.

7. It is Not About You

Interpreting is a communications business. As an interpreter, you are part of a broader conversation, and complete neutrality remains a lofty yet elusive aspiration. Try as you might you cannot help but bring into the picture some of your true essence. It will show through in your intonation, your word choice, the length of your pauses, even. You are certainly not at liberty to share your opinions in the booth, but the interaction will be different because of you. That is OK. But only as long as you can shift the focus away from you.

You are not a translation machine. Think communicate, rather than interpret, and don't be afraid to contribute the attributes that make you a unique enabler. But remember that good communicators make it all about their interlocutors. Good interpreters take a genuine interest in those on the receiving end.

Take-home point: they are happy that you are there for them, but they are not there for you.

GEAR

Portable Equipment: What to Get and Why

Portable interpretation systems get a bad rap, and the names used to designate them leave no doubt: tour-guide system; *bidule* (the thingy); *valisette* (the briefcase).

Yet there are settings where they are the only practical solution available, which explains their increasing popularity with many international organizations for use on field missions and in meeting rooms that would not accommodate a large booth. And for the convenience and affordability these devices provide, private market clients are getting hooked on them, too.

True, in the old days the standard portable equipment could subject the interpreter to long hours of standing and poor sound quality. With the typical tour-guide system, the interpreter, having no direct audio feed, had to rely on natural hearing, which meant moving about the room to ensure everyone taking the floor was well within earshot. The interpreter also needed to speak extra softly, so that his voice would not override that of the speaker by whom he stood. Not the best working conditions.

Well, those days are gone. A new generation of

portable equipment has solved these issues. The latest systems allow the interpreter to listen to crystal clear incoming audio and deliver his or her interpretation from a seat at the back of the room.

And should there be more speakers around the table — like in a small boardroom fitted with conference microphones or a lecture hall with a few handheld mics — a dock station or a fixed transmitter can be added that captures any audio feed going through the PA and channels it wirelessly to the interpreter.

So, no more leaning onto speakers and walking about disruptively in order to hear. No more whispering (or chuchotage) either. As for the participants, they can elect to listen to the speaker or the interpreter, choosing the corresponding channel on their battery-operated, compact receivers.

These new systems are affordable and will give you good service for many years. They are also a buy that will quickly pay for itself. It will increase your employability as more clients will be drawn to you if they know you have the right hardware. You can also capitalize on your portable set by leasing it out to other colleagues.

So, if you are an interpreter and you don't yet have portable equipment, I would strongly advise that you invest in some. Williams Sound has a neat bi-directional system that you may consider if your budget is not too tight. I have distributed the brand for many years, and it is very reliable.

A more affordable option I really like is the new system by Media-Vision. Receivers are very compact, sound quality is amazing, and you can accommodate everything in a light-weight briefcase with a built-in battery charger that is easy to carry on and off flights.

There are other decent brands out there, so be sure to do a search online. If you don't know where to look or don't have the time, let me know, and I will try to steer you in the right direction.

Two final considerations, by way of disclaimer, before I go:

1. A portable equipment is neither suitable for all circumstances, nor meant to replace high-end conference equipment required for large conferences. It is not supposed to question the value of proper consecutive interpretation at high-level diplomatic or commercial bilateral meetings.

2. As a conscientious interpreter, you must continue to enforce the working conditions our profession has fought so hard to establish, especially with regard to manning strength and workload. No equipment in the world should replace that.

That said, a reliable portable equipment can be a lifesaver during field missions or if you are called to handle small meetings or presentations. It did save mine on more than one occasion

.

Portable Equipment Tips

If you are an interpreter, chances are you have already used or will soon have to use portable interpretation equipment, a.k.a. tour-guide system —a set of portable transmitters and wireless receivers commonly used for the purposes of guided tours (hence the name) and... oh, yes, interpretation.

I used to distribute those gadgets, and I have also used them extensively. Although they look very straightforward, there are things to be aware of. I have compiled below a list of useful recommendations that you may want to keep in mind when using such equipment for the first couple of times.

The specifics

Whenever possible, choose transmitters that feature a 'mute' button (e.g., William Sound's PFM T36). Make sure you know how to operate the mute button. Beware not to turn off the unit inadvertently. On that model, the two switches (mute and on/off) are identical, and they are very close to one another.

Use the mute button only if you need to, in case

you absolutely need to clear your throat, say something urgent or drink water. Use discretion in determining what's urgent.

If you're stuck with a transmitter that does not have a mute button, accept it as a fact of life and hang in there. Whatever you do, don't turn the unit off without first warning the delegates, as this will produce a terrible hissing sound that can even damage their ears.

Also, do not try unplugging your microphone as an alternative way to circumvent the lack of a mute button. If you absolutely must cough or clear or throat, gently unclip your mic(or take off your headset), move it away from you (again, very gently), do whatever you need to do and then put everything back on after you're done. But do try to limit such occurrences to an absolute minimum.

Whenever possible, choose the headset microphone that leaves your ears free (e.g., model MIC 096). They look like a simple wire without any sort of ear pads. They are also adjusted with a powerful compressor, which significantly reduces ambient noise when you are speaking, allowing you to speak very softly.

If you are stuck with the older models (the ones with padded ears), place them as you would normally do and then slightly uncover your ears, so you can hear naturally. Do not leave the headset hanging around your neck. This will cause your voice to fade in and out, depending on where you turn your head. It will also pick up a lot of unwanted noises from friction against your collar or other clothing items.

Be careful when clipping your microphone or adjusting your headset. Run a little test beforehand (with the help of a colleague), to check for optimal mic positioning, and then leave it at that. If you are using the lapel mic, make sure they are not rubbing against your tie, your coat, necklaces, etc. If you are using one of the headsets, make sure it's placed close to your mouth (although not too close) and away from your nostrils (you don't want it picking up your breathing, especially if you're under stress).

Save for the situation described in item 3, above, keep your hands off the mic at all times. These microphones are very sensitive. Touching them produces very unpleasant noise. Also, refrain from scratching your beard or your hair, and try not to lip smack. By all means, repress your sighs of relief and use the mute button to swallow any liquid.

If you need to take turns with your colleague during the session, make sure to mute the unit as you hand the receiver over. Ideally, two different transmitters should be used (both of which on the same frequency).

When switching with a colleague, eye contact is key. The interpreter who is idle should get ready and silently inform the other of his/her preparedness. The one who's speaking should then signal that he/she is about to turn off his/her unit, at the end of a given sentence. Now here's the trick: The interpreter who's getting ready to go has to switch his/her unit on a split second before the colleague who's leaving turns his/her off.

When the session is over, or when it breaks for coffee or so, you may want to turn your transmitter off. Before you do so, please advise delegates of your intention and give them time to take their earpieces off. Make sure to make your announcement in both languages and wait for a second while scanning the room to make sure nobody will be disturbed by the hiss.

Feel free to move about. When you work with portable equipment without audio feedback into your headset, you depend on your natural hearing abilities. Before the session begins, let delegates and speakers know that you may on occasion have to approach them.

However, as you move about the room, make sure to do so in a very unobtrusive manner and in such a way as not to get in anyone's way. Don't come too close to people or rush across the room to approach whoever is speaking. And by all means don't interrupt them by saying `wait, wait… I can't hear you, can you please speak up?!` Approach people gracefully, and do the best you can, while keeping as composed as possible. If by any chance something important escapes you, make that known gently to the delegates who are listening to your interpretation. You may say something like "the interpreter is not certain to have heard well. Please let me know whether you want that repeated". Then let the delegate choose whether any reiteration is needed.

As you interact, remember to keep eye contact. You're there to communicate. You're part of the meeting. And if they are really using too soft a tone of voice, make that known to the delegates using the equipment.

> ***Important:*** *never leave two transmitters on at the same time, as they will cancel each other out.*

> ***Very important:*** *make sure your transmitter is off during the breaks and after the session. This is hard to do with the older models, as they have no LED to indicate they're on. My advice is that you unplug your mic from it, to be sure, especially if you're using the restroom.*

That about covers the most important aspects.

Please be gentle on yourself. Mastering the use of

portable equipment is harder than it looks. It takes practice and time. Now, I know the list above can be overwhelming. Please go only as far as you can without compromising your natural delivery and interpretation style. These recommendations are meant as mere reminders. Work on those that make sense to you.

I hope this helps. Good luck.

A Cool Portable Equipment Hack

If you enjoyed the discussion on the value of portable interpretation equipment, you will probably like this cool equipment hack.

It introduces a rather creative way to use the *bidule*, whenever the number of people in the audience exceeds the number of receivers available. This came about as a quick fix during a mission in Sao Tome and Principe, back a decade or so.

We were asked to interpret into Portuguese a series of presentations by the mission team. In the audience were about 40 top government officials from STP. The problem was we only had 12 receivers. Consecutive interpretation would prove tedious and hard to squeeze into the limited time slot we had.

We had to improvise, so here's what I did:

Instead of distributing headphones and receivers to the audience, I gave those gadgets to the six officials on our team. And instead of giving speakers a standard mic, I had them talk through one of the portable interpretation transmitters.

Wearing a portable receiver as feed, I stood on

stage and interpreted the presentations simultaneously into a stand-up microphone. The lusophone audience heard it all in Portuguese through the PA system. The rest of our delegation listened to the English original on a different channel on their receivers. Now, ain't that a cool equipment hack?

Speakers were still in front of the crowd, speaking from the podium, with their message coming through the loudspeakers already in crystal-clear Portuguese.

The groundbreaking, patent-pending technique, modestly dubbed the Magellan Protocol (or MagPro for short), will certainly take the world of interpreting by storm, and word has it that the Royal Swedish Academy of Sciences is now considering the introduction of a new Nobel Prize category that will carry twice the usual compensation.

I'm sitting by the phone. And I can assure you that unlike Bob I will return their calls promptly and hop on the first plane to Stockholm to grab that check.

TIPS FOR SPEAKERS

What Interpreters Can Tell Speakers About Speaking

Speakers come in two basic varieties: those who shine and those who struggle. The difference in what they do is subtle. The gap in their impact is huge.

In this age of ubiquitous information and instant interactivity, the ability to communicate well has gone from being a desirable professional attribute to being a crucial life skill. Professional and personal advancement is inextricably linked with how effectively and persuasively one can get in front of people and convey ideas that will inspire others to act.

Speaking engagements pop up often at school, at church, during job interviews and staff meetings. They are career and leadership opportunities in disguise and, as such, should not be wasted.

For over 20 years, I have shared the stage with speakers of all stripes. I have lent them my voice, paraphrased their words and scrutinized their mannerisms for the thinnest slices of meaning. Making sense of speakers is what I do for a living as a conference interpreter.

As it turns out, speakers can only indirectly gauge the impact of their presence. Interpreters, by contrast, are uniquely placed between the stage and the audience, as close to presenters as they are to the public.

Interpreters are skilled rapport builders, sounding boards trained to spot and compensate for their interlocutors' shortcomings. Prolific speakers in our own right, we play different roles at once and approach public speaking from many different angles. We hold an important piece to the puzzle.

After 30 years as a conference interpreter, making sense of speakers becomes second nature. It is easy to see what works and what doesn't.

Regrettably, most presenters adhere to a predictable presentation script that goes like this:

- open with a busy overview slide
- cover every item in an orderly fashion
- finish with a painful recap of every bullet covered

They basically tell you how they plan to bore you, then they bore you, and they show you how they did it.

This is an old-school approach that some would consider safe. But is it wise?

Bored minds crave excitement, not structure. Telling people what to expect eliminates the one ingredient that could keep attendees glued to their seats all along: *suspense*. It also conditions people to be selective in how they give their attention: *Oh, I will look up again when she reaches bullet 9. In the meantime, let me check my Facebook feed and pretend I am tweeting about the talk.*

The Language Game

At the end of the day, the inability to anticipate what a speaker will say —and the hope that he or she will say something worth one's salt— is what keeps people listening through the end of a talk. It is also what keeps interpreters up the night before, and engaged at their peak performance the following morning once the microphone is on. They know that once a speaker is off the cuff, anything can happen and that redemption will come only by committing their undivided attention —if it comes at all.

By contrast, spoon-feeding an audience too much information too soon may lead to complacency. Familiarity breeds contempt.

While hard facts and figures are key to our understanding and appraisal of reality, only through stories do our minds begin to assign meaning to the information we receive. We are all born into a language and, just as well, into a particular canon of oral tradition. As humans, we are hardwired to communicate orally. Language is an instinctive drive, a life skill. Our ancestors were accomplished storytellers way before they put together the first alphabet or string of numbers.

We learn to speak by listening and repeating stories passed on for generations. Through tales heard and shared, we affirm the identity that makes us unique while looking for the commonalities that make us all human. Writing and math, as precious and useful as they are, came late in our evolutionary trail. First, it was the voice, the spoken word! We are born storytellers. We long to tell and be told stories.

An able speaker understands this basic human longing. She knows people won't gather around a bonfire for a recital of figures or a budget review. They come for the story and will leave —or get detached— once it fades away.

Weaving stories into a talk is a fail-safe way of ensuring increased appreciation and retention of a message. Nobody has the formula, but here are seven things I have seen used with good results.

1. Open with a challenging claim or the promise of an a-ha moment: *What if everything you knew about X was wrong?*

2. Pique people's curiosity through a few more odd claims. Work on your pauses to allow them time to ponder. A curious mind will agree to temporarily move beyond plausibility and follow you down a rabbit hole.

3. Use analogies and imagery to help people digest numbers and stats. Don't bother saying a nanometer is 10 to the power of minus 9. Tell them it is as long as their fingernails will grow in one second. It is equally elusive, but it will get them looking at the back of their hands and away from their phones.

4. Engage their senses. Give them something to hear, smell, touch, and taste in their mind. Use language allusive to color, music, texture, flavor, and fragrance.

5. Engage their emotions, too, by appealing to the humorous, sad, or hopeful side of your tale. Make it human.

6. Make it personal. Put the audience in the picture or give them someone or something they can root for.

7. Remove yourself from the frame and become just

the narrator. It is the story they care about.

Don't try it all at once. Prepare a good opening tale for your next talk, with at least three of the ingredients above and give it a try. It may not bring the house down, but I guarantee it will take you further than your sad bulleted list would.

Speaking Abroad?
Here's the Cheat Sheet

If you are speaking abroad, chances are people will not be listening to you. Rather, they will be listening to an interpreter. Sure, it all depends on the country and the dominant language where you're going, but at some point, somewhere, it will happen to you.

Now, aren't professional interpreters trained to handle the most complex speeches and different speaking styles? Should you bother?

Yes, you should. Interpreters are resourceful communicators and will go out of their way so that you make as much sense in their language as you do in your own. They sharpen their tools constantly and will aptly handle their precision instruments to ensure you come across as you must. Yet, there are many variables they do not control. They can't anticipate what you are going to say, and they don't get to edit your words after the talk. You can trust them to give their best so that you wow your audience. But they only get one shot at it. If only you could help (sigh!)

As it turns out, you can. With the right attitude, there are a few simple things you can do before, during, and after the conference to help interpreters do you justice. Here's the cheat sheet:

Before the conference

- Ask that your contact info be shared with the interpreters. Make it easy for them to contact you.

- Share with your interpreters in advance any material that you think would help them prepare (e.g., presentations, speeches, or videos).

- Bring hard copies of your speaking notes and bio for the interpreters. A pen drive with your PowerPoint may come in handy, too.

- Agree to a five-minute meeting with your interpreters, to update them on any last-minute changes, share documents or give them a heads up on your jokes.

- Use font, colors, and shapes that are legible and clear for those in the very back of the room. This is where your interpreters will be.

- Run a quick sound check to make sure the interpreters can hear and be heard well and get acquainted with any equipment you may need to use and wear (e.g., headset).

During the presentation

- Leave your slides on-screen a few seconds longer than usual, so interpreters have a chance to finish reading any relevant information.

- Get used to a longer-than-usual delay in audience

response. Interpreters are often a few words behind you. Note that those not relying on interpreters may react first. Laughs and applause will come in waves, and that is OK.

- Always speak into the microphone, even if you are addressing a specific person in the audience. Remember that the person may only be able to hear you through the interpreter.

- Don't bother repeating to the audience questions or comments heard in your own language. The interpreters will have done it for you.

- Important: Always turn off a lapel mic when you leave the room, especially if you plan to use the restroom.

After the conference

- Give interpreters your honest feedback. They are always looking for ways to improve. Do it in writing, if you can.

- Invite their feedback. I am sure you are also looking for ways to improve.

This should give your interpreters —and yourself— the peace of mind required to concentrate on form as well as content.

Follow these simple steps, and I guarantee your ideas will be rendered as precisely and eloquently as intended, in any language.

BIBLIOGRAPHY

ARANHA, Maria Lúcia A. & MARTINS, Maria Helena P. (1993). *Filosofando: Introdução à Filosofia*. São Paulo: Editora Moderna.

BACELAR, Laura. (2002). *Escreva seu livro*. São Paulo: Editora Mercuryo.

BERGREEN, Laurence. (2003). Over the Edge of the World. Magellan's Terrifying Circumnavigation of the Globe. New York: HarperCollins Publishers.

BERLITZ, Charles. (1982). *As línguas do mundo*. Translated by Heloísa Gonçalves Barbosa. Rio de Janeiro: Editora Nova Fronteira.

BLACKBURN, Simon. (1997). *Dicionário Oxford de Filosofia*. Translated by Desidério Murcho. Rio de Janeiro: Jorge Zahar Editor.

CAMPOS, Geir. (1986). *O que é tradução?* São Paulo: Editora Brasiliense.

CARPINETTI, Luis Carlos L. (2003). *O aspecto polêmico da apologia de Jerônimo contra Rufino*. Doctoral dissertation. São Paulo: Faculdade de Filosofia, Letras e Ciências Humanas. Universidade de São Paulo.

DAHOUI, Albert Paul. (2005). *O sucesso de escrever* (electronic version). São Paulo: Editora Corifeu.

DELISLE, Jean and WOODSWORTH, Judith (orgs.). (2005). *Translators in History*. Amsterdam: John Benjamins-Unesco Publishing.

DOLLERUP, Cay and LODDEGAARD, Anne (orgs.). (1992). *Teaching Translation and Interpreting: Training Talent and Experience*. First International Conference on Languages in Elsinore, Denmark, 1991. Amsterdam: John Benjamins.

GAMBIER, Yves, GILE, Daniel and TAYLOR, Christopher (orgs.). (1997). *Conference Interpreting: Current Trends in Research*: Proceedings of the International Conference on Interpreting: What Do We Know and How? Amsterdam: John Benjamins.

GILE, Daniel. (1995). *Basic Concepts and Models for Interpreter and Translator Training*. Amsterdam: John Benjamins.

GLADWELL, Malcolm. (2003). *Blink*. The power of thinking without thinking. New York: Back Bay Books.

GRICE, Paul H. (1989). *Studies in the Way of Words*. Cambridge: Harvard University Press.

KRAKAUER, Jon. (1998). *Into Thin Air: A personal account of the Mount Everest disaster*. New York: Random House, Inc.

LYNCH, Dudley and KORDIS, Paul. (1990). *The Strategy of the Dolphin*. New York: Random House Publishing Group.

MAGALHAES, Ewandro. (2007). *Sua Majestade, o Intérprete. O Fascinante mundo da tradução simultânea*. São Paulo: Parábola Editorial.

OAKLEY, Kenneth P. (1961). *Man, The Toolmaker*. London: Jarrolds and Sons.

ORWELL, George. (1949). *1984*. London: Secker and Warburg.

PERSICO, Joseph E. (1995). *Nuremberg: Infamy on Trial.* New York, Penguin Books.

PINKER, Steven. (1995). *The Language Instinct. How the Mind Creates Language.* New York: HarperPerennial Edition.

ROCHA, Everardo. (1985). *O que é Mito.* São Paulo: Editora Brasiliense.

SÁNCHEZ, Vasquez A. (1998). *Ética.* Translated by João Dell'Anna. Rio de Janeiro: Editora Civilização Brasileira.

SETTON, Robin and DAWRANT, Andrew. (2016). *Conference Interpreting. A trainer's guide.* Amsterdam: John Benjamins.

SETTON, Robin and DAWRANT, Andrew. (2016). *Conference Interpreting. A complete course.* Amsterdam: John Benjamins.

SONTAG, Susan. (2003). *O evangelho hegemônico da tradução.* Translated by Bluma Waddington Vilar. Retrieved from www.folha.com.br.

St. JEROME. *Letter to Pammachius, on the best method of translating.* Letter 57. Retrieved from www.newadvent.org.

CHI-TING, Chuang and KEARNS, Patrick. (2001). *Communication Error Behind Crash.* Retrieved from www.taipeitimes.com.

TUSA, Ann and TUSA, John. (2003). *The Nuremberg Trials.*

Natl. Book Network.

VARGAS LLOSA, Mario. (2008). *The Bad Girl*. Translated by Edith Grossman. New York: Picador.

VIAGGIO, Sergio. *The Tribulations of a Chief Interpreter*. Retrieved from https://aiic.net.

VIANNA, Branca. *Teoria da relevância e interpretação*. Retrieved from https://aiic.net.

Acknowledgments

The act of writing often implies hours of immobility where nothing gets done, despite pages and pages of text, and intense, productive days spent in fast-paced thinking without a single word committed to paper. It is a solitary act.

The act of composing a book, by contrast, implies the hopeful anticipation that someone will be out there to read it, and an early realization that nothing ever gets done without help. It is a collective endeavor, a dream we share with many other people.

I am indebted to a large lot of people. Yet naming every individual who helped me get here and who made this book possible would most likely double the word count and transcend the patience of the most loyal reader.

My heart is filled with gratitude for every colleague, professor, mentor friend, family, critic, and competitor who helped me forge my character and create a career for myself. I know who they are and the contribution they made. They know I know, and whenever practical, I have expressed my gratitude to them individually, in different forms.

And I also have you to thank, for picking up this book and for caring to hear what I had to say.

About the Author

Ewandro is a seasoned conference interpreter with over 27 years of experience. He is the former Chief Interpreter of ITU, a specialized agency of the United Nations with headquarters in Geneva, Switzerland. He is a contractor with the US Department of State, IMF, World Bank, PAHO, OAS, and other multilateral organizations. Ewandro has interpreted for five Brazilian presidents, two American presidents, and countless heads of State government.

He is a TEDx speaker and author, and his TED Lessons have been viewed over a million times. He is the author of *Sua Majestade, o Intérprete: o Fascinante Mundo da Interpretação Simultânea*, the first book ever written about the craft of interpreting in the Portuguese language and a reference in the field. He also contributes numerous articles to specialized journals and publication in the

Translation and Interpretation field.

Ewandro offers intensive group and individual coaching sessions for interpreters interested in boosting their careers and increasing their visibility. To learn more about his courses and engage his coaching or speaking services, please visit **www.ewandro.com**

Ewandro speaks four languages in addition to his native Portuguese. He can and often does present in English, Portuguese, French, and Spanish. A retired triathlete and marathon runner, Ewandro keeps active on his bike and at the gym. A national of Brazil, he has lived on three continents before settling in Manhattan with his wife and Freddie, the family's Yorkie. They have three children and one lovely grandchild.

Made in the USA
Middletown, DE
21 September 2023